COMPTIA®
SECURITY+
SYO-401 Q&A

CHIMBORAZO PUBLISHING INC.

Cengage Learning PTR

CENGAGE
Learning®

Professional • Technical • Reference

Australia, Brazil, Japan, Korea, Mexico, Singapore, Spain, United Kingdom, United States

Professional • Technical • Reference

CompTIA® Security+ SY0-401 Q&A
Chimborazo Publishing Inc.

Publisher and General Manager,
Cengage Learning PTR:
Stacy L. Hiquet

Manager of Editorial Services:
Heather Talbot

Product Team Manager:
Heather Hurley

Technical Editor:
Danielle Shaw

Interior Layout Tech:
Bill Hartman

Cover Designer:
Mike Tanamachi

Proofreader:
Jenny Davidson

Cover image:
© everything possible/Shutterstock.com

For product information and technology assistance, contact us at
Cengage Learning Customer & Sales Support, 1-800-354-9706

For permission to use material from this text or product,
submit all requests online at **cengage.com/permissions**
Further permissions questions can be emailed to
permissionrequest@cengage.com

Library of Congress Control Number: 2015934616

ISBN-13: 978-1-305-51144-6

ISBN-10: 1-305-51144-1

Cengage Learning PTR
20 Channel Center Street
Boston, MA 02210
USA

Cengage Learning is a leading provider of customized learning solutions
with office locations around the globe, including Singapore, the United
Kingdom, Australia, Mexico, Brazil, and Japan. Locate your local office at:
international.cengage.com/region

Cengage Learning products are represented in Canada by Nelson
Education, Ltd.

For your lifelong learning solutions, visit **cengageptr.com**

Visit our corporate website at cengage.com

Printed in the United States of America
Print Number: 01   Print Year: 2015

ABOUT THE AUTHOR

Chimborazo Publishing, Inc. specializes in content development for courses, texts, and instructor/student resources at the college, trade, and high school level, and in a wide range of disciplines. These products include testbanks, instructor manuals, presentations, scenario- and project-based learning modules, and course objectives and curriculum design. All Chimborazo subject matter experts have advanced degrees and extensive experience with teaching and in industry.

CONTENTS

Part I

CompTIA Security+ EXAM SY0-401

Domain 1.0 Network Security

Domain 2.0 Compliance and Operational Security

Domain 3.0 Threats and Vulnerabilities

Domain 4.0 Application, Data, and Host Security

Domain 5.0 Access Control and Identity Management

Domain 6.0 Cryptography

1.0

NETWORK SECURITY

TEST PREPARATION QUESTIONS

1. What is the primary role of a firewall?

   A. To forward packets across different network computer networks

   B. To intercept user requests from the internal secure network and then process that request on behalf of the user

   C. To connect networks together so that they function as a single network segment

   D. To inspect packets and either accept or deny entry

   Security+ SY0-401 Objective 1.1: Implement security configuration parameters on network devices and other technologies.

   REF: 7-280

2. Which type of firewall packet filtering looks at the incoming packet and permits or denies it based on the conditions that have been set by the administrator?

   A. Stateless packet filtering

   B. Stateful packet filtering

   C. Switched packet filtering

   D. Secure packet filtering

   Security+ SY0-401 Objective 1.1: Implement security configuration parameters on network devices and other technologies.

   REF: 7-280

3. When a modern firewall receives a packet, it tends to use a(n) _____ method to determine the action to be taken.

A. rule-based

B. role-based

C. application-based

D. authentication-based

Security+ SY0-401 Objective 1.1: Implement security configuration parameters on network devices and other technologies.

REF: 7-281

4. What type of firewall systems are static in nature and cannot do anything other than what they have been expressly configured to do?

A. Application-based

B. Authentication-based

C. Role-based

D. Rule-based

Security+ SY0-401 Objective 1.1: Implement security configuration parameters on network devices and other technologies.

REF: 7-281

5. What is the role of a router?

A. To inspect packets and either accept or deny entry

B. To forward packets across different computer networks

C. To intercept user requests from the internal secure network and then process that request on behalf of the user

D. To connect networks together so that they function as a single network segment

Security+ SY0-401 Objective 1.1: Implement security configuration parameters on network devices and other technologies.

REF: 7-276

6. What is the role of a switch?

A. To inspect packets and either accept or deny entry

B. To forward packets across different network computer networks

C. To intercept user requests from the internal secure network and then process that request on behalf of the user

D. To connect networks together so that they function as a single network segment

Security+ SY0-401 Objective 1.1: Implement security configuration parameters on network devices and other technologies.

REF: 7-274

7. Which type of switch network monitoring is best suited for high-speed networks that have a large volume of traffic?

   A. Network tapping

   B. Port mirroring

   C. Load balancing

   D. Packet filtering

   Security+ SY0–401 Objective 1.1: Implement security configuration parameters on network devices and other technologies.

   REF: 7-276

8. A load balancer is typically located _____ in a network configuration.

   A. in front of a server

   B. in front of a router

   C. between a router and a server

   D. between a router and a switch

   Security+ SY0–401 Objective 1.1: Implement security configuration parameters on network devices and other technologies.

   REF: 7-277

9. Load balancing that is used for distributing HTTP requests received is sometimes called _____.

   A. content filtering

   B. IP spraying

   C. content inspection

   D. port mirroring

   Security+ SY0–401 Objective 1.1: Implement security configuration parameters on network devices and other technologies.

   REF: 7-277

10. A(n) _____ is a computer or an application program that intercepts user requests from the internal secure network and then processes that request on behalf of the user.

    A. proxy server

    B. load balancer

    C. network tap

    D. Internet content filter

    Security+ SY0–401 Objective 1.1: Implement security configuration parameters on network devices and other technologies.

    REF: 7-277

11. A(n) _____ can block malicious content in real time as it appears.

    A. uniform resource locator (URL) filter

    B. virtual private network (VPN)

    C. Internet content filter

    D. web security gateway

    Security+ SY0-401 Objective 1.1: Implement security configuration parameters on network devices and other technologies.

    REF: 7-285

12. What term refers to a technology that enables authorized users to use an unsecured public network, such as the Internet, as if it were a secure private network?

    A. Virtual private network (VPN)

    B. Gateway

    C. Intrusion detection system (IDS)

    D. Port mirroring

    Security+ SY0-401 Objective 1.1: Implement security configuration parameters on network devices and other technologies.

    REF: 7-284

13. VPN transmissions are achieved through communicating with _____.

    A. network taps

    B. endpoints

    C. Internet content filters

    D. proxy servers

    Security+ SY0-401 Objective 1.1: Implement security configuration parameters on network devices and other technologies.

    REF: 7-284

14. Which statement concerning behavior-based monitoring is correct?

    A. It is necessary to update signature files before monitoring can take place.

    B. It is necessary to compile a baseline of statistical behavior before monitoring can take place.

    C. It can more quickly stop new attacks as compared to anomaly- and behavior-based monitoring.

    D. Behavior-based monitoring operates in a reactive mode.

    Security+ SY0-401 Objective 1.1: Implement security configuration parameters on network devices and other technologies.

    REF: 7-286

15. Which statement concerning signature-based monitoring is correct?
    A. Signature-based monitoring is designed for detecting statistical anomalies.
    B. Signature-based monitoring uses an algorithm to determine if a threat exists.
    C. Signature-based monitoring operates by being adaptive and proactive.
    D. Signature-based monitoring looks for well-known patterns.
    Security+ SY0-401 Objective 1.1: Implement security configuration parameters on network devices and other technologies.
    REF: 7-286

16. Which statement concerning anomaly-based monitoring is correct?
    A. Anomaly-based monitoring is founded on experience based techniques.
    B. Anomaly-based monitoring looks for well-known patterns.
    C. Anomaly-based monitoring operates by being adaptive and proactive.
    D. Anomaly-based monitoring is designed for detecting statistical anomalies.
    Security+ SY0-401 Objective 1.1: Implement security configuration parameters on network devices and other technologies.
    REF: 7-286

17. Which statement concerning heuristic monitoring is correct?
    A. Heuristic monitoring operates by being adaptive and proactive.
    B. Heuristic monitoring is founded on experience-based techniques.
    C. Heuristic monitoring is designed for detecting statistical anomalies.
    D. Heuristic monitoring looks for well-known patterns.
    Security+ SY0-401 Objective 1.1: Implement security configuration parameters on network devices and other technologies.
    REF: 7-287

18. A(n) _____ captures packets to decode and analyzes their contents.
    A. protocol analyzer
    B. load balancer
    C. Internet content filter
    D. spam filter
    Security+ SY0-401 Objective 1.1: Implement security configuration parameters on network devices and other technologies.
    REF: 7-274

19. Which option for installing a corporate spam filter is considered to be the most effective approach?

    A. Install the spam filter on the Domain Name Server (DNS).

    B. Install the spam filter on the Post Office Protocol (POP3) server.

    C. Install the spam filter with the Simple Mail Transfer Protocol (SMTP) server.

    D. Contract with a third-party entity that filters out spam.

    Security+ SY0-401 Objective 1.1: Implement security configuration parameters on network devices and other technologies.

    REF: 7-282

20. Which type of Internet content filtering restricts unapproved websites from being displayed by searching for and matching keywords?

    A. Uniform resource locator (URL filtering)

    B. Profiling

    C. Malware inspection

    D. Content inspection

    Security+ SY0-401 Objective 1.1: Implement security configuration parameters on network devices and other technologies.

    REF: 7-285

21. Using _____, filters can assess if a webpage contains any malicious elements or exhibits any malicious behavior, and then flag questionable pages with a warning message.

    A. malware inspection and filtering

    B. content inspection

    C. uniform resource locator (URL) filtering

    D. detailed reporting

    Security+ SY0-401 Objective 1.1: Implement security configuration parameters on network devices and other technologies.

    REF: 7-285

22. A _____ is a special type of firewall that looks at the applications using HTTP.

    A. network intrusion detection system (NIDS)

    B. network intrusion prevention system (NIPS)

    C. spam filter

    D. web application firewall

    Security+ SY0-401 Objective 1.1: Implement security configuration parameters on network devices and other technologies.

    REF: 7-281

23. A more "intelligent" firewall is a(n) _____ firewall, sometimes called a next-generation firewall (NGFW).

A. rule-based

B. application–aware

C. hardware-based

D. host-based

Security+ SY0–401 Objective 1.1: Implement security configuration parameters on network devices and other technologies.

REF: 7-281

24. What feature distinguishes a network intrusion prevention system (NIPS) from a network intrusion detection system (NIDS)?

A. A NIPS has sensors that monitor the traffic entering and leaving a firewall, and reports back to the central device for analysis.

B. A NIPS is located "in line" on the firewall itself.

C. A NIPS is designed to integrate with existing antivirus, antispyware, and firewalls that are installed on the local host computer.

D. A NIPS can use a protocol stack verification technique.

Security+ SY0–401 Objective 1.1: Implement security configuration parameters on network devices and other technologies.

REF: 7-289

25. Which statement concerning a network intrusion detection system (NIDS) is correct?

A. A NIDS knows such information as the applications that are running as well as the underlying operating systems so that it can provide a higher degree of accuracy regarding potential attacks.

B. Compared to a network intrusion prevention system (NIPS), a NIDS can more quickly take action to block and attack.

C. A NIDS attempts prevent malicious attacks by stopping the attack.

D. A NIDS has sensors that monitor the traffic entering and leaving a firewall, and reports back to the central device for analysis.

Security+ SY0–401 Objective 1.1: Implement security configuration parameters on network devices and other technologies.

REF: 7-288

26. Each firewall rule is essentially a separate instruction with a(n) _____ construction.

    A. FOR-EACH

    B. DO-UNTIL

    C. IF-THEN

    D. WHILE-DO

    Security+ SY0-401 Objective 1.2: Given a scenario, use secure network administration principles.

    REF: 7-281

27. Within a firewall rule, the _____ describes the TCP/IP port number being used to send packets of data through.

    A. source port

    B. destination port

    C. source address

    D. destination address

    Security+ SY0-401 Objective 1.2: Given a scenario, use secure network administration principles.

    REF: 7-281

28. What statement accurately describes a best practice for managing a virtual LAN (VLAN)?

    A. Configure empty switch ports to connect to a used VLAN.

    B. Keep all default VLAN names.

    C. Configure the ports on the switch that pass tagged VLAN packets to explicitly forward specific tags.

    D. Configure VLANs so that public devices are on a private VLAN.

    Security+ SY0-401 Objective 1.2: Given a scenario, use secure network administration principles.

    REF: 8-331

29. Which statement represents a best practice for securing router configurations?

    A. Allow remote configuration for dynamic installation in case of an emergency.

    B. Store the router configuration on a public network for easy access in case of an emergency.

    C. Store the router configuration on a USB drive for compact storage.

    D. Perform changes in the router configuration from the console.

    Security+ SY0-401 Objective 1.2: Given a scenario, use secure network administration principles.

    REF: 8-326

30. Which statement accurately describes an access control list characteristic?

    A. Access control lists are efficient.

    B. Access control lists are simple to manage in an enterprise setting.

    C. The structure behind an access control list table can be complex.

    D. Access control lists are used extensively with UNIX systems but not on Windows operating systems.

    Security+ SY0-401 Objective 1.2: Given a scenario, use secure network administration principles.

    REF: 11-454

31. Ports can be secured through disabling unused interfaces, using _____, and through IEEE 802.1x.

    A. media access control (MAC) limiting and filtering

    B. virtual private network (VPN) tunneling

    C. packet sniffers

    D. virtual local area networks (VLANs)

    Security+ SY0-401 Objective 1.2: Given a scenario, use secure network administration principles.

    REF: 8-332

32. The IEEE 802.1x standard provides the highest degree of port security by implementing port-based _____.

    A. encryption

    B. authentication

    C. auditing

    D. integrity

    Security+ SY0-401 Objective 1.2: Given a scenario, use secure network administration principles.

    REF: 8-332

33. A _____ is a feature that controls a device's tolerance for unanswered service requests and helps to prevent a denial of service (DoS) attack.

    A. flood guard

    B. virtual local area network (VLAN)

    C. network intrusion detection system (NIDS)

    D. virtual private network (VPN) concentrator

    Security+ SY0-401 Objective 1.2: Given a scenario, use secure network administration principles.

    REF: 8-327

34. _____ can be prevented with loop protection.

    A. IP address spoofing

    B. Man-in-the-middle attacks

    C. Denial of service (DoS) attacks

    D. Broadcast storms

    Security+ SY0-401 Objective 1.2: Given a scenario, use secure network administration principles.

    REF: 8-330

35. Loop protection uses the _____ standard spanning-tree algorithm (STA).

    A. IEEE 801.2d

    B. IEEE 802.3

    C. IEEE 802.11n

    D. IEEE 802.1d

    Security+ SY0-401 Objective 1.2: Given a scenario, use secure network administration principles.

    REF: 8-330

36. _____ in access control means that if a condition is not explicitly met, the request for access is rejected.

    A. Static allow

    B. Explicit allow

    C. Implicit deny

    D. Dynamic deny

    Security+ SY0-401 Objective 1.2: Given a scenario, use secure network administration principles.

    REF: 11-453

37. One way to provide network separation is to physically separate users by connecting them to different _____.

    A. switches and routers

    B. hubs

    C. mirrored ports

    D. operating systems

    Security+ SY0-401 Objective 1.2: Given a scenario, use secure network administration principles.

    REF: 8-330

38. A security _____ log can provide details regarding requests for specific files on a system.

    A. event

    B. administration

    C. audit

    D. access

    Security+ SY0-401 Objective 1.2: Given a scenario, use secure network administration principles.

    REF: 8-327

39. What item is considered to be the biggest obstacle to log management?

    A. Offsite storage accessibility

    B. Very large volume of data

    C. Multiple devices generating logs

    D. Different log formats

    Security+ SY0-401 Objective 1.2: Given a scenario, use secure network administration principles.

    REF: 8-329

40. An integrated device that combines several security functions is called a(n) _____ security product.

    A. demilitarized zone (DMZ)

    B. unified threat management (UTM)

    C. virtual private network (VPN)

    D. application-aware IPS

    Security+ SY0-401 Objective 1.2: Given a scenario, use secure network administration principles.

    REF: 7-289

41. A _____ functions as a separate network that rests outside the secure network perimeter.

    A. gateway

    B. segment

    C. virtual private network (VPN)

    D. demilitarized zone (DMZ)

    Security+ SY0-401 Objective 1.3: Explain network design elements and components.

    REF: 7-293

42. Allowing an IP address to be split anywhere within its 32 bits is known as
    _____.
    A. splitting
    B. spanning
    C. subnetting
    D. IP spraying
    Security+ SY0-401 Objective 1.3: Explain network design elements and components.
    REF: 7-293

43. With subnetting, rather than simply having networks and hosts, networks can effectively be divided into three parts: _____.
    A. network, subnet, and port
    B. port, subnet, and IP address
    C. network, port, and host
    D. network, subnet, and host
    Security+ SY0-401 Objective 1.3: Explain network design elements and components.
    REF: 7-293

44. Networks are usually segmented by using _____ to divide the network
    into a hierarchy.
    A. hubs
    B. routers
    C. switches
    D. proxies
    Security+ SY0-401 Objective 1.3: Explain network design elements and components.
    REF: 7-296

45. _____ switches reside at the top of the hierarchy and carry traffic between
    switches, while _____ switches are connected directly to the devices on
    the network.
    A. Workgroup; core
    B. Core; workgroup
    C. Public; private
    D. Private; public
    Security+ SY0-401 Objective 1.3: Explain network design elements and components.
    REF: 7-296

46. Segmenting a network by separating devices into logical groups is known as creating a _____.
    A. cloud
    B. virtual LAN (VLAN)
    C. flood guard
    D. unified threat management (UTM) system
    Security+ SY0-401 Objective 1.3: Explain network design elements and components.
    REF: 7-296

47. Which term describes a technique that allows private IP addresses to be used on the public Internet?
    A. Network address translation (NAT)
    B. Port address translation (PAT)
    C. Network access control (NAC)
    D. Loop protection
    Security+ SY0-401 Objective 1.3: Explain network design elements and components.
    REF: 7-290

48. By using _____, instead of giving each outgoing packet a different IP address, each packet is given the same IP address but a different TCP port number.
    A. port address translation (PAT)
    B. network access control (NAC)
    C. network address translation (NAT)
    D. port mirroring
    Security+ SY0-401 Objective 1.3: Explain network design elements and components.
    REF: 7-290

49. _____ refers to any combination of hardware and software that enables remote users to access a local internal network.
    A. Virtual LAN (VLAN) management
    B. Cloud computing
    C. Unified threat management (UTM)
    D. Remote access
    Security+ SY0-401 Objective 1.3: Explain network design elements and components.
    REF: 7-297

50. Which term describes the concept of using a data based IP network to add digital voice clients and new voice applications onto the IP network?

    A. IP telephony

    B. Virtualization

    C. Loop protection

    D. Captive portals

    Security+ SY0-401 Objective 1.3: Explain network design elements and components.
    REF: 8-334

51. Which statement accurately describes IP telephony?

    A. IP telephony requires an increase in infrastructure requirements.

    B. IP telephony convergence provides the functionality of managing and supporting a single network for all applications.

    C. New IP telephony applications can take a long time to develop.

    D. The cost of convergence technologies is high in comparison to startup costs for new traditional telephone equipment.

    Security+ SY0-401 Objective 1.3: Explain network design elements and components.
    REF: 8-334

52. The goal of _____ is to prevent computers with suboptimal security from potentially infecting other computers through the network.

    A. network access control (NAC)

    B. virtualization

    C. captive portals

    D. port security

    Security+ SY0-401 Objective 1.3: Explain network design elements and components.
    REF: 7-291

53. Which term describes a means of managing and presenting computer resources by function without regard to their physical layout or location?

    A. Port mirroring

    B. Virtualization

    C. Cloud computing

    D. Virtual LAN (VLAN) management

    Security+ SY0-401 Objective 1.3: Explain network design elements and components.
    REF: 8-335

54. In _____ virtualization, an entire operating system environment is simulated.

   A. host

   B. network

   C. application

   D. cloud

   Security+ SY0-401 Objective 1.3: Explain network design elements and components.
   REF: 8-335

55. Which term refers to the expansion and contraction of random access memory (RAM) or hard drive space as needed?

   A. On-demand computing

   B. Host computing

   C. Host availability

   D. Host elasticity

   Security+ SY0-401 Objective 1.3: Explain network design elements and components.
   REF: 8-336

56. Which term refers to a pay-per-use computing model in which customers pay only for the online computing resources they need?

   A. Host computing

   B. Cloud computing

   C. Patch computing

   D. Server computing

   Security+ SY0-401 Objective 1.3: Explain network design elements and components.
   REF: 8-337

57. Which cloud computing service model allows the consumer to install and run their own specialized applications on the cloud computing network without requiring the consumer to manage or configure any of the underlying cloud infrastructure?

   A. Application as a Service (AaaS)

   B. Infrastructure as a Service (IaaS)

   C. Software as a Service (SaaS)

   D. Platform as a Service (PaaS)

   Security+ SY0-401 Objective 1.3: Explain network design elements and components.
   REF: 8-339

58. In the _____ model, the cloud computing vendor provides access to the vendor's software applications running on a cloud infrastructure.
    A. Infrastructure as a Service (IaaS)
    B. Application as a Service (AaaS)
    C. Software as a Service (SaaS)
    D. Platform as a Service (PaaS)
    Security+ SY0-401 Objective 1.3: Explain network design elements and components.
    REF: 8-338

59. Which cloud computing service model provides the customer the highest level of control?
    A. Application as a Service (AaaS)
    B. Software as a Service (SaaS)
    C. Platform as a Service (PaaS)
    D. Infrastructure as a Service (IaaS)
    Security+ SY0-401 Objective 1.3: Explain network design elements and components.
    REF: 8-339

60. A _____ cloud offers the highest level of security and control.
    A. public
    B. community
    C. private
    D. hybrid
    Security+ SY0-401 Objective 1.3: Explain network design elements and components.
    REF: 8-338

61. A _____ cloud is one in which the services and infrastructure are offered to all users with access provided remotely through the Internet.
    A. private
    B. public
    C. hybrid
    D. community
    Security+ SY0-401 Objective 1.3: Explain network design elements and components.
    REF: 8-338

62. A _____ cloud is a combination of public and private clouds.
    A. community
    B. hybrid
    C. mixed
    D. connected
    Security+ SY0-401 Objective 1.3: Explain network design elements and components.
    REF: 8-335

63. A _____ cloud is a cloud that is open only to specific organizations that have common concerns.

    A. community

    B. public

    C. hybrid

    D. private

    Security+ SY0-401 Objective 1.3: Explain network design elements and components.

    REF: 8-338

64. Another name for layered security is _____.

    A. network separation

    B. VPN tunneling

    C. Unified threat management (UTM)

    D. defense in depth

    Security+ SY0-401 Objective 1.3: Explain network design elements and components.

    REF: 7-272

65. _____ is a protocol suite for securing Internet Protocol (IP) communications.

    A. Internet Small Computer System Interface (iSCSI)

    B. Internet Control Message Protocol (ICMP)

    C. Internet Protocol Security (IPsec)

    D. Hypertext Transport Protocol Secure (HTTPS)

    Security+ SY0-401 Objective 1.4: Given a scenario, implement common protocols and services.

    REF: 6-251

66. What two encryption modes are supported by Internet Protocol Security (IPsec)?

    A. Electronic code book (ECB) and cipher block chaining (CBC)

    B. Kerberos and Secure Shell (SSH)

    C. Secure Sockets Layer (SSL) and Transport Layer Security (TLS)

    D. Transport and tunnel

    Security+ SY0-401 Objective 1.4: Given a scenario, implement common protocols and services.

    REF: 6-252

67. Which protocol is used to manage network equipment and is supported by most network equipment manufacturers?

    A. Simple Network Management Protocol (SNMP)

    B. Internet Control Message Protocol (ICMP)

    C. Secure Copy Protocol (SCP)

    D. Transmission Control Protocol/Internet Protocol (TCP/IP)

    Security+ SY0-401 Objective 1.4: Given a scenario, implement common protocols and services.

    REF: 8-316

68. _____ is an encrypted alternative to the Telnet protocol that is used to access remote computers.

    A. Internet Control Message Protocol (ICMP)

    B. Internet Small Computer System Interface (iSCSI)

    C. Secure Shell (SSH)

    D. Secure Network Management Protocol (SNMP)

    Security+ SY0-401 Objective 1.4: Given a scenario, implement common protocols and services.

    REF: 6-250

69. Which protocol is a TCP/IP protocol that resolves (maps) a symbolic name (www.cengage.com) with its corresponding IP address (69.32.133.11)?

    A. Internet protocol (IP)

    B. Internet Control Message Protocol (ICMP)

    C. Domain Name System (DNS)

    D. Hypertext Transport Protocol Secure (HTTPS)

    Security+ SY0-401 Objective 1.4: Given a scenario, implement common protocols and services.

    REF: 8-317

70. A newer secure version of DNS known as _____ allows DNS information to be digitally signed so that an attacker cannot forge DNS information.

    A. Domain Name System Security (DNSS)

    B. Advanced Domain Name System (ADNS)

    C. Domain Name System2 (DNS2)

    D. Domain Name System Security Extensions (DNSSEC)

    Security+ SY0-401 Objective 1.4: Given a scenario, implement common protocols and services.

    REF: 8-318

71. _____ is a cryptographic transport algorithm.

   A. Secure Shell (SSH)

   B. Data Encryption Standard (DES)

   C. Advanced Encryption Standard (AES)

   D. Transport Layer Security (TLS)

   Security+ SY0-401 Objective 1.4: Given a scenario, implement common protocols and services.

   REF: 6-249

72. Which common cryptographic transport algorithm was developed by Netscape in 1994 in response to the growing concern over Internet security?

   A. Hypertext Transport Protocol Secure (HTTPS)

   B. Secure Shell (SSH)

   C. Secure Sockets Layer (SSL)

   D. Transport Layer Security (TLS)

   Security+ SY0-401 Objective 1.4: Given a scenario, implement common protocols and services.

   REF: 6-249

73. What is the most common protocol used today for both local area networks (LANs) and the Internet?

   A. Transmission Control Protocol/Internet Protocol (TCP/IP)

   B. Secure Sockets Layer (SSL)

   C. Hypertext Transport Protocol Secure (HTTPS)

   D. Domain Name System (DNS)

   Security+ SY0-401 Objective 1.4: Given a scenario, implement common protocols and services.

   REF: 8-313

74. TCP/IP uses its own four-layer architecture that includes _____ layers.

   A. Network Interface, Internet, Transport, and Application

   B. Network Interface, Network, Transport, and Application

   C. Network Interface, Internet, Transport, and Authentication

   D. Network Interface, Network, Transport, and Authentication

   Security+ SY0-401 Objective 1.4: Given a scenario, implement common protocols and services.

   REF: 8-314

75. Which statement accurately describes a characteristic of FTP Secure (FTPS)?

    A. FTPS is an entire protocol itself.

    B. FTPS is a combination of two technologies (FTP and SSL or TLS).

    C. FTPS uses a single TCP port.

    D. FTPS encrypts and compresses all data and commands.

    Security+ SY0-401 Objective 1.4: Given a scenario, implement common protocols and services.

    REF: 8-320

76. A weakness of FTPS is that although the control port commands are encrypted, the data port (_____) may or may not be encrypted.

    A. port 20

    B. port 21

    C. port 25

    D. port 80

    Security+ SY0-401 Objective 1.4: Given a scenario, implement common protocols and services.

    REF: 8-320

77. Which protocol uses TLS and SSL to secure Hypertext Transport Protocol (HTTP) communications between a browser and a web server?

    A. FTP Secure (FTPS)

    B. Secure Shell (SSH)

    C. Hypertext Transport Protocol Secure (HTTPS)

    D. Internet Protocol Security (IPsec)

    Security+ SY0-401 Objective 1.4: Given a scenario, implement common protocols and services.

    REF: 6-251

78. Which protocol is used for file transfers?

    A. Internet Small Computer System Interface (iSCSI)

    B. Network Basic Input/Output System (NetBIOS)

    C. Secure Network Management Protocol (SNMP)

    D. Secure Copy Protocol (SCP)

    Security+ SY0-401 Objective 1.4: Given a scenario, implement common protocols and services.

    REF: 8-320

79. Which statement describes a limitation of Secure Copy Protocol (SCP)?

    A. SCP can only operate in the Windows environment.

    B. SCP cannot encrypt commands.

    C. SCP is being replaced by Remote Copy Protocol (RCP).

    D. A file transfer cannot be interrupted and then resumed in the same session.

    Security+ SY0-401 Objective 1.4: Given a scenario, implement common protocols and services.

    REF: 8-320

80. Communications between different IP devices on a network is handled by one of the core protocols of TCP/IP, namely, _____.

    A. Internet Control Message Protocol (ICMP)

    B. Network Basic Input/Output System (NetBIOS)

    C. Telnet

    D. Simple Network Management Protocol (SNMP)

    Security+ SY0-401 Objective 1.4: Given a scenario, implement common protocols and services.

    REF: 8-314

81. In a(n) _____ attack, an Internet Control Message Protocol (ICMP) redirect packet is sent to the victim that asks the host to send its packets to another "router," which is actually a malicious device.

    A. network discovery

    B. smurf

    C. ICMP redirect

    D. ping of death

    Security+ SY0-401 Objective 1.4: Given a scenario, implement common protocols and services.

    REF: 8-316

82. In a(n) _____ attack, a malformed ICMP ping that exceeds the size of an IP packet is sent to the victim's computer potentially causing the host to crash.

    A. network discovery

    B. smurf

    C. ICMP redirect

    D. ping of death

    Security+ SY0-401 Objective 1.4: Given a scenario, implement common protocols and services.

    REF: 8-316

83. An Internet Protocol version 4 (IPv4) address is _____ in length.
    A. 64 bits
    B. 64 bytes
    C. 32 bytes
    D. 32 bits
    Security+ SY0-401 Objective 1.4: Given a scenario, implement common protocols and services.
    REF: 8-324

84. An Internet Protocol version 6 (IPv6) address is _____ in length.
    A. 128 bits
    B. 64 bytes
    C. 32 bytes
    D. 32 bits
    Security+ SY0-401 Objective 1.4: Given a scenario, implement common protocols and services.
    REF: 8-325

85. _____ is an IP-based storage networking standard for linking data storage facilities.
    A. Internet Small Computer System Interface (iSCSI)
    B. Internet Control Message Protocol (ICMP)
    C. Simple Network Management Protocol (SNMP)
    D. Network Basic Input/Output System (NetBIOS)
    Security+ SY0-401 Objective 1.4: Given a scenario, implement common protocols and services.
    REF: 8-321

86. Fiber channel (FC) is a high-speed storage network protocol that can transmit up to _____ per second.
    A. 16 bits
    B. 16 megabits
    C. 16 gigabits
    D. 16 terabits
    Security+ SY0-401 Objective 1.4: Given a scenario, implement common protocols and services.
    REF: 8-321

87. Fibre Channel over Ethernet (FCoE) encapsulates Fibre Channel _____ over Ethernet networks.

    A. headers

    B. addresses

    C. frames

    D. packets

    Security+ SY0-401 Objective 1.4: Given a scenario, implement common protocols.

    REF: 8-321

88. Transferring files can be performed using the File Transfer Protocol (FTP), which is a(n) _____ TCP/IP protocol.

    A. unsecure

    B. secure

    C. open

    D. closed

    Security+ SY0-401 Objective 1.4: Given a scenario, implement common protocols and services.

    REF: 8-318

89. Which statement accurately describes Secure FTP (SFTP)?

    A. SFTP is a combination of two technologies (FTP and SSL or TLS).

    B. SFTP uses two ports.

    C. SFTP is an entire protocol itself.

    D. SFTP encrypts and compresses only data, not commands.

    Security+ SY0-401 Objective 1.4: Given a scenario, implement common protocols and services.

    REF: 8-320

90. Which protocol is often used for the automated transfer of configuration files between devices?

    A. Hypertext Transfer Protocol (HTTP)

    B. Secure Copy Protocol (SCP)

    C. Trivial File Transfer Protocol (TFTP)

    D. Secure FTP (SFTP)

    Security+ SY0-401 Objective 1.4: Given a scenario, implement common protocols and services.

    REF: 8-318

91. Which term describes both an older TCP/IP protocol for text-based communication and a terminal emulation program?

    A. Telnet

    B. File Transfer Protocol (FTP)

    C. Network Basic Input/Output System (NetBIOS)

    D. Secure Network Management Protocol (SNMP)

    Security+ SY0-401 Objective 1.4: Given a scenario, implement common protocols and services.

    REF: 8-323

92. Which protocol is the standard protocol for Internet usage?

    A. Internet Control Message Protocol (ICMP)

    B. Hypertext Transport Protocol (HTTP)

    C. Network Basic Input/Output System (NetBIOS)

    D. Secure Network Management Protocol (SNMP)

    Security+ SY0-401 Objective 1.4: Given a scenario, implement common protocols and services.

    REF: 2-65

93. NetBIOS (Network Basic Input/Output System) is a transport protocol used by _____ systems to allow applications on separate computers to communicate over a LAN.

    A. Microsoft Windows

    B. Linux

    C. Apple

    D. Unix

    Security+ SY0-401 Objective 1.4: Given a scenario, implement common protocols and services.

    REF: 8-323

94. Which port does the File Transfer Protocol (FTP) use for commands?

    A. 20

    B. 21

    C. 22

    D. 25

    Security+ SY0-401 Objective 1.4: Given a scenario, implement common protocols and services.

    REF: 15-615

95. Which port does the Secure Shell (SSH) protocol use?

    A. 21

    B. 22

    C. 139

    D. 443

    Security+ SY0-401 Objective 1.4: Given a scenario, implement common protocols and services.

    REF: 15-615

96. Which port does the Simple Mail Transfer Protocol (SMTP) use?

    A. 25

    B. 53

    C. 110

    D. 143

    Security+ SY0-401 Objective 1.4: Given a scenario, implement common protocols and services.

    REF: 15-615

97. Which port does the Domain Name System (DNS) protocol use?

    A. 25

    B. 53

    C. 80

    D. 443

    Security+ SY0-401 Objective 1.4: Given a scenario, implement common protocols and services.

    REF: 15-615

98. Which port does the Hypertext Transfer Protocol (HTTP) use?

    A. 20

    B. 21

    C. 80

    D. 443

    Security+ SY0-401 Objective 1.4: Given a scenario, implement common protocols and services.

    REF: 15-615

1

99. Which port does the Post Office Protocol v3 (POP3) use?

    A. 22

    B. 25

    C. 80

    D. 110

    Security+ SY0-401 Objective 1.4: Given a scenario, implement common protocols and services.

    REF: 15-615

100. Which port does NetBIOS use?

    A. 80

    B. 139

    C. 143

    D. 443

    Security+ SY0-401 Objective 1.4: Given a scenario, implement common protocols and services.

    REF: 15-615

101. Which port does the Internet Message Access Protocol (IMAP) use?

    A. 25

    B. 143

    C. 443

    D. 3389

    Security+ SY0-401 Objective 1.4: Given a scenario, implement common protocols and services.

    REF: 15-615

102. Which port does the Hypertext Transfer Protocol Secure (HTTPS) use?

    A. 53

    B. 143

    C. 443

    D. 3389

    Security+ SY0-401 Objective 1.4: Given a scenario, implement common protocols and services.

    REF: 15-615

103. Which port does the Microsoft Terminal Server use?

    A. 53

    B. 143

    C. 443

    D. 3389

    Security+ SY0-401 Objective 1.4: Given a scenario, implement common protocols and services.

    REF: 15-615

104. TCP/IP uses its own _____ architecture that corresponds generally to the OSI reference model.

    A. two-layer

    B. three-layer

    C. four-layer

    D. seven-layer

    Security+ SY0-401 Objective 1.4: Given a scenario, implement common protocols and services.

    REF: 8-314

105. There are two modes for Wi-Fi Protected Access (WPA): _____.

    A. WPA Personal and WPA Enterprise

    B. WPA Private and WPA Public

    C. WPA Open and WPA Closed

    D. WPA Shortwave and WPA Longwave

    Security+ SY0-401 Objective 1.5: Given a scenario, troubleshoot security issues related to wireless networking.

    REF: 9-380

106. What are the two major security areas of WLANs addressed by WPA2?

    A. Access and integrity

    B. Encryption and authentication

    C. Encryption and access

    D. Authentication and access

    Security+ SY0-401 Objective 1.5: Given a scenario, troubleshoot security issues related to wireless networking.

    REF: 9-382

107. _____ is an IEEE 802.11 security protocol designed to ensure that only authorized parties can view transmitted wireless information.

A. PSK2-mixed mode

B. Temporal Key Integrity Protocol (TKIP)

C. Wired Equivalent Privacy (WEP)

D. Extensible Authentication Protocol (EAP)

Security+ SY0-401 Objective 1.5: Given a scenario, troubleshoot security issues related to wireless networking.

REF: 9-376

108. _____ was created as a more secure alternative than the weak Challenge Handshake Authentication Protocol (CHAP) and Password Authentication Protocol (PAP).

A. Temporal Key Integrity Protocol (TKIP)

B. Advanced Encryption Standard (AES)

C. Protected EAP (PEAP)

D. Extensible Authentication Protocol (EAP)

Security+ SY0-401 Objective 1.5: Given a scenario, troubleshoot security issues related to wireless networking.

REF: 9-383

109. _____ is designed to simplify the deployment of 802.1x by using Microsoft Windows logins and passwords.

A. Protected EAP (PEAP)

B. Lightweight EAP (LEAP)

C. Temporal Key Integrity Protocol (TKIP)

D. PSK2-mixed mode

Security+ SY0-401 Objective 1.5: Given a scenario, troubleshoot security issues related to wireless networking.

REF: 9-383

110. _____ is a proprietary EAP method developed by Cisco Systems and is based on the Microsoft implementation of Challenge Handshake Authentication Protocol (CHAP).

A. Lightweight EAP (LEAP)

B. Advanced Encryption Standard (AES)

C. Protected EAP (PEAP)

D. Temporal Key Integrity Protocol (TKIP)

Security+ SY0-401 Objective 1.5: Given a scenario, troubleshoot security issues related to wireless networking.

REF: 9-383

111. What is the most common type of wireless access control?
    A. Electronic Access Control (EAC)
    B. Media Access Control (MAC) address filtering
    C. Extensible Authentication Protocol-Transport Layer Security (EAP/TLS)
    D. Port Based Access Control (PBAC)

    Security+ SY0-401 Objective 1.5: Given a scenario, troubleshoot security issues related to wireless networking.
    REF: 9-377

112. Which statement accurately describes a weakness in disabling SSID broadcasts?
    A. Turning off the SSID broadcast may allow users to freely roam from one AP coverage area to another.
    B. For most hardware routers, the effect is temporary and the disabling actions must be repeated frequently.
    C. Disabling SSID broadcasts may disable the entire network.
    D. Attackers with protocol analyzers can still detect the SSID.

    Security+ SY0-401 Objective 1.5: Given a scenario, troubleshoot security issues related to wireless networking.
    REF: 9-379

113. The heart and soul of WPA is a newer encryption technology called _____.
    A. Temporal Key Integrity Protocol (TKIP)
    B. Advanced Encryption Standard (AES)
    C. Triple DES
    D. Counter Mode with Cipher Block Chaining Message Authentication Code Protocol (CCMP)

    Security+ SY0-401 Objective 1.5: Given a scenario, troubleshoot security issues related to wireless networking.
    REF: 9-380

114. The encryption protocol used for WPA2 is the _____.
    A. Triple DES
    B. Advanced Encryption Standard (AES)
    C. Counter Mode with Cipher Block Chaining Message Authentication Code Protocol (CCMP)
    D. Temporal Key Integrity Protocol (TKIP)

    Security+ SY0-401 Objective 1.5: Given a scenario, troubleshoot security issues related to wireless networking.
    REF: 9-382

115. Why do experts recommend that access points (APs) be mounted as high as possible?

    A. Antennas must hang upside down for best performance.

    B. The radio frequency (RF) signal may experience fewer obstructions.

    C. The air is "heavier" as it rises, providing better transmission of the radio frequency (RF) signal.

    D. Warm air rises and provides a better conductor for the radio frequency (RF) signal.

    Security+ SY0-401 Objective 1.5: Given a scenario, troubleshoot security issues related to wireless networking.

    REF: 9-386

116. What is the advantage of using an access point's (AP's) power level control?

    A. The power can be adjusted to "jam" frequencies of sniffers used by potential hackers.

    B. The power can be adjusted to provide a cleaner signal with less interference.

    C. The power can be adjusted so that more of the signal leaves the premises and reaches outsiders.

    D. The power can be adjusted so that less of the signal leaves the premises and reaches outsiders.

    Security+ SY0-401 Objective 1.5: Given a scenario, troubleshoot security issues related to wireless networking.

    REF: 9-385

117. A(n) _____ access point (AP) uses a standard web browser to provide information, and gives the wireless user the opportunity to agree to a policy or present valid login credentials, providing a higher degree of security.

    A. captive portal

    B. open portal

    C. closed portal

    D. Internet portal

    Security+ SY0-401 Objective 1.5: Given a scenario, troubleshoot security issues related to wireless networking.

    REF: 9-384

118. All wireless network interface card (NIC) adapters have _____ antennas.

    A. external

    B. peripheral

    C. embedded

    D. focused

    Security+ SY0-401 Objective 1.5: Given a scenario, troubleshoot security issues related to wireless networking.

    REF: 9-375

119. A(n) _____ is an in-depth examination and analysis of a wireless LAN site.

A. network log

B. site survey

C. captive portal

D. threat vector

Security+ SY0-401 Objective 1.5: Given a scenario, troubleshoot security issues related to wireless networking.

REF: 9-386

120. A(n) _____ VPN, often used on mobile devices like laptops in which the VPN endpoint is actually software running on the device itself, offers the most flexibility in how network traffic is managed.

A. closed

B. open

C. hardware-based

D. software-based

Security+ SY0-401 Objective 1.5: Given a scenario, troubleshoot security issues related to wireless networking.

REF: 7-285

2.0

COMPLIANCE AND OPERATIONAL SECURITY

2

TEST PREPARATION QUESTIONS

1. Risk _____ involves identifying the risk, but making a decision to not engage in the activity.
   A. deterrence
   B. mitigation
   C. acceptance
   D. avoidance
   Security+ SY0-401 Objective 2.1: Explain the importance of risk related concepts.
   REF: 1-17

2. Risk _____ simply means that the risk is acknowledged but that no steps are taken to address it.
   A. deterrence
   B. mitigation
   C. acceptance
   D. avoidance
   Security+ SY0-401 Objective 2.1: Explain the importance of risk related concepts.
   REF: 1-17

3. Risk _____ is the attempt to address risks by making risk less serious.

A. deterrence

B. mitigation

C. acceptance

D. avoidance

Security+ SY0-401 Objective 2.1: Explain the importance of risk related concepts.

REF: 1-17

4. Risk _____ involves understanding something about the attacker and then informing him of the harm that may come his way if he attacks an asset.

A. deterrence

B. mitigation

C. transference

D. avoidance

Security+ SY0-401 Objective 2.1: Explain the importance of risk related concepts.

REF: 1-17

5. The term risk _____ refers to the act of shifting risk to a third party.

A. deterrence

B. mitigation

C. transference

D. avoidance

Security+ SY0-401 Objective 2.1: Explain the importance of risk related concepts.

REF: 1-17

6. Which statement concerning virtualized environments is correct?

A. Existing security tools, such as antivirus, antispam, and IDS, are designed for single physical servers and do not always adapt well to multiple virtual machines.

B. All hypervisors have the necessary security controls to keep out determined attackers.

C. In a network with virtual machines, external devices such as firewalls and IDS reside between servers and can help prevent one from infecting another.

D. A guest operating system that has remained dormant for a period of time can contain the latest patches and other security updates.

Security+ SY0-401 Objective 2.1: Explain the importance of risk related concepts.

REF: 8-337

7. With _____, the customer's data should be properly isolated from that of other customers, and the highest level of application availability and security must be maintained.

   A. virtualization

   B. IP telephony

   C. Sandboxing

   D. cloud computing

   Security+ SY0-401 Objective 2.1: Explain the importance of risk related concepts.

   REF: 8-339

8. One of the best practices for access control is _____, which requires that if the fraudulent application of a process might potentially result in a breach of security, the process should be divided between two or more individuals.

   A. job rotation

   B. mandatory vacation

   C. separation of duties

   D. least privilege

   Security+ SY0-401 Objective 2.1: Explain the importance of risk related concepts.

   REF: 11-451

9. An advantage of _____ is that it helps to expose any potential avenues for fraud by having multiple individuals with different perspectives learn about the job and uncover vulnerabilities that someone else may have overlooked.

   A. job rotation

   B. mandatory vacation

   C. separation of duties

   D. least privilege

   Security+ SY0-401 Objective 2.1: Explain the importance of risk related concepts.

   REF: 11-451

10. _____ limits the amount of time that individuals have to manipulate security configurations.

    A. Job rotation

    B. Mandatory vacation

    C. Separation of duties

    D. Least privilege

    Security+ SY0-401 Objective 2.1: Explain the importance of risk related concepts.

    REF: 11-451

11. Limiting access to rooms in a building is a model of the information technology security principle of _____.

    A. job rotation

    B. mandatory vacations

    C. separation of duties

    D. least privilege

    Security+ SY0-401 Objective 2.1: Explain the importance of risk related concepts.

    REF: 11-452

12. In many fraud schemes, the perpetrator must be present every day in order to continue the fraud or keep it from being exposed. Many organizations require _____ for all employees to counteract this.

    A. job rotation

    B. mandatory vacations

    C. separation of duties

    D. least privilege

    Security+ SY0-401 Objective 2.1: Explain the importance of risk related concepts.

    REF: 11-453

13. In redundancy and fault tolerance, the term _____ describes the average amount of time that it will take a device to recover from a failure that is not a terminal failure.

    A. mean time to recovery

    B. failure In Time

    C. mean time between failures

    D. mean time to failure

    Security+ SY0-401 Objective 2.1: Explain the importance of risk related concepts.

    REF: 13-530

14. The term _____ refers to the average (mean) amount of time until a component fails, cannot be repaired, and must be replaced.

    A. mean time to recovery

    B. failure in time

    C. mean time between failures

    D. mean time to failure

    Security+ SY0-401 Objective 2.1: Explain the importance of risk related concepts.

    REF: 13-531

15. The _____ is the maximum length of time that an organization can tolerate between backups.

    A. mean time to failure

    B. recovery point objective

    C. mean time to recovery

    D. recovery time objective

    Security+ SY0-401 Objective 2.1: Explain the importance of risk related concepts.

    REF: 13-538

16. The _____ is the length of time it will take to recover the data that has been backed up.

    A. mean time to recovery

    B. recovery point objective

    C. mean time to failure

    D. recovery time objective

    Security+ SY0-401 Objective 2.1: Explain the importance of risk related concepts.

    REF: 13-538

17. An event that, in the beginning, is considered to be a risk, yet turns out not to be one, is called a _____.

    A. false negative

    B. false positive

    C. negative-positive

    D. positive-negative

    Security+ SY0-401 Objective 2.1: Explain the importance of risk related concepts.

    REF: 14-568

18. A _____ is an event that does not appear to be a risk but actually turns out to be one.

    A. false positive

    B. negative-positive

    C. false negative

    D. positive-negative

    Security+ SY0-401 Objective 2.1: Explain the importance of risk related concepts.

    REF: 14-568

2

19. Which type of risk control is administrative in nature and includes the laws, regulations, policies, practices, and guidelines that govern overall requirements and controls?

    A. Technical

    B. System

    C. Management

    D. Operational

    Security+ SY0-401 Objective 2.1: Explain the importance of risk related concepts.

    REF: 14-569

20. Which type of risk control involves enforcing technology to control risk, such as antivirus software, firewalls, and encryption?

    A. Technical

    B. System

    C. Management

    D. Operational

    Security+ SY0-401 Objective 2.1: Explain the importance of risk related concepts.

    REF: 14-569

21. Which type of risk control may include using video surveillance systems and barricades to limit access to secure sites?

    A. Technical

    B. System

    C. Management

    D. Operational

    Security+ SY0-401 Objective 2.1: Explain the importance of risk related concepts.

    REF: 14-569

22. The _____ approach to calculating risk uses an "educated guess" based on observation.

    A. cumulative

    B. qualitative

    C. technical

    D. quantitative

    Security+ SY0-401 Objective 2.1: Explain the importance of risk related concepts.

    REF: 14-572

23. The _____ approach to calculating risk attempts to create "hard" numbers associated with the risk of an element in a system by using historical data.
    A. cumulative
    B. qualitative
    C. technical
    D. quantitative
    Security+ SY0-401 Objective 2.1: Explain the importance of risk related concepts.
    REF: 14-572

24. What is the average amount of time expected until the first failure of a piece of equipment?
    A. Mean Time to Recovery
    B. Failure In Time
    C. Mean Time Between Failures
    D. Mean Time To Failure
    Security+ SY0-401 Objective 2.1: Explain the importance of risk related concepts.
    REF: 14-573

25. Historical data can be used to determine the likelihood of a risk occurring within a year. This is known as the _____.
    A. Annualized Loss Expectancy
    B. Single Loss Expectancy
    C. Multiple Loss Expectancy
    D. Annualized Rate of Occurrence
    Security+ SY0-401 Objective 2.1: Explain the importance of risk related concepts.
    REF: 14-573

26. The _____ is the expected monetary loss that can be expected for an asset due to a risk over a one-year period.
    A. Single Loss Expectancy
    B. Annualized Rate of Occurrence
    C. Annualized Loss Expectancy
    D. Multiple Loss Expectancy
    Security+ SY0-401 Objective 2.1: Explain the importance of risk related concepts.
    REF: 14-574

2

27. Consider a building with a value of $10,000,000 (AV) of which 75 percent of it is likely to be destroyed by a tornado (EF). The SLE is _____.

    A. $7,500

    B. $75,000

    C. $750,000

    D. $7,500,000

    Security+ SY0-401 Objective 2.1: Explain the importance of risk related concepts.

    REF: 14-574

28. The _____ is the expected monetary loss every time a risk occurs.

    A. Annualized Loss Expectancy

    B. Single Loss Expectancy

    C. Annualized Rate of Occurrence

    D. Multiple Loss Expectancy

    Security+ SY0-401 Objective 2.1: Explain the importance of risk related concepts.

    REF: 14-574

29. What is a written document that states how an organization plans to protect the company's information technology assets?

    A. Privacy notice

    B. Acceptable use

    C. Security policy

    D. Data insurance

    Security+ SY0-401 Objective 2.1: Explain the importance of risk related concepts.

    REF: 14-575

30. What two key elements must be carefully balanced in an effective security policy?

    A. Trust and control

    B. Due process and due care

    C. Due process and due diligence

    D. Privilege and threat

    Security+ SY0-401 Objective 2.1: Explain the importance of risk related concepts.

    REF: 14-575

31. A(n) _____ policy outlines how the organization uses the personal information it collects.

    A. acceptable use

    B. privacy

    C. data acquisition

    D. data storage

    Security+ SY0-401 Objective 2.1: Explain the importance of risk related concepts.

    REF: 14-581

32. A(n) _____ policy is one that defines the actions users may perform while accessing systems and networking equipment.

    A. data acquisition

    B. privacy

    C. data storage

    D. acceptable use

    Security+ SY0-401 Objective 2.1: Explain the importance of risk related concepts.

    REF: 14-581

33. _____ business partners refers to the start-up relationship between partners.

    A. Enrolling

    B. On-boarding

    C. Unrolling

    D. Off-boarding

    Security+ SY0-401 Objective 2.2: Summarize the security implications of integrating systems and data with third parties.

    REF: 15-625

34. A(n) _____ is a service contract between a vendor and a client that specifies what services will be provided, the responsibilities of each party, and any guarantees of service.

    A. Service Level Agreement

    B. Memorandum of Understanding

    C. Blanket Purchase Agreement

    D. Interconnection Security Agreement

    Security+ SY0-401 Objective 2.2: Summarize the security implications of integrating systems and data with third parties.

    REF: 15-625

35. A(n) _____ is a prearranged purchase or sale agreement between a government agency and a business.

    A. Service Level Agreement

    B. Memorandum of Understanding

    C. Blanket Purchase Agreement

    D. Interconnection Security Agreement

    Security+ SY0-401 Objective 2.2: Summarize the security implications of integrating systems and data with third parties.

    REF: 15-625

2

36. A(n) _____ demonstrates a "convergence of will" between the parties so that they can work together.
    A. Service Level Agreement
    B. Memorandum of Understanding
    C. Blanket Purchase Agreement
    D. Interconnection Security Agreement
    Security+ SY0-401 Objective 2.2: Summarize the security implications of integrating systems and data with third parties.
    REF: 15-625

37. A(n) _____ is an agreement that is intended to minimize security risks for data transmitted across a network.
    A. Service Level Agreement
    B. Memorandum of Understanding
    C. Blanket Purchase Agreement
    D. Interconnection Security Agreement
    Security+ SY0-401 Objective 2.2: Summarize the security implications of integrating systems and data with third parties.
    REF: 15-625

38. The term _____ business partners refers to the termination of an agreement between parties.
    A. enrolling
    B. on-boarding
    C. unrolling
    D. off-boarding
    Security+ SY0-401 Objective 2.2: Summarize the security implications of integrating systems and data with third parties.
    REF: 15-625

39. One of the means by which the parties can reach an understanding of their relationships and responsibilities is through _____, particularly as they relate to security policy and procedures.
    A. security agreements
    B. baseline agreements
    C. interoperability agreements
    D. intrusive vulnerability agreements
    Security+ SY0-401 Objective 2.2: Summarize the security implications of integrating systems and data with third parties.
    REF: 15-625

40. What system of security tools is used to recognize and identify data that is critical to the organization and to ensure that it is protected?

    A. Data loss prevention

    B. Corrective control

    C. Compensating control

    D. Bayesian filtering

    Security+ SY0-401 Objective 2.3: Given a scenario, implement appropriate risk mitigation strategies.

    REF: 4-161

41. _____ serve to verify that the organization's security protections are being enacted and that corrective actions can be swiftly implemented before an attacker exploits a vulnerability.

    A. Audits

    B. Use policies

    C. Data policies

    D. Risk calculations

    Security+ SY0-401 Objective 2.3: Given a scenario, implement appropriate risk mitigation strategies.

    REF: 14-570

42. One element of privilege management is periodic review of a subject's privileges over an object, known as _____.

    A. peer auditing

    B. privilege auditing

    C. privilege review

    D. privilege profiling

    Security+ SY0-401 Objective 2.3: Given a scenario, implement appropriate risk mitigation strategies.

    REF: 14-570

43. _____ refers to a methodology for making modifications and keeping track of those changes.

    A. Risk management

    B. Data management

    C. Incident management

    D. Change management

    Security+ SY0-401 Objective 2.3: Given a scenario, implement appropriate risk mitigation strategies.

    REF: 14-571

2

44. The objective of _____ is to restore normal operations as quickly as possible with the least possible impact on either the business or the users.

A. risk management

B. data management

C. incident management

D. change management

Security+ SY0-401 Objective 2.3: Given a scenario, implement appropriate risk mitigation strategies.

REF: 14-572

45. If your forensics response team is external to the organization, it is important that they accurately track their _____ from the start of the investigation to verify their involvement.

A. hours and expenses

B. contract responsibilities

C. staff's location

D. equipments' serial numbers

Security+ SY0-401 Objective 2.4: Given a scenario, implement basic forensic procedures.

REF: 13-546

46. _____ involves documenting the physical surroundings of the computer with video; interviewing witnesses; and taking photographs of images displayed on the screen.

A. Establishing a chain of custody

B. Initiating damage control

C. Securing a crime scene

D. Examining the evidence

Security+ SY0-401 Objective 2.4: Given a scenario, implement basic forensic procedures.

REF: 13-545

47. The term _____ is used to describe the sequence of volatile data that must be preserved in a computer forensic investigation.

A. hot site

B. chain of custody

C. system image

D. order of volatility

Security+ SY0-401 Objective 2.4: Given a scenario, implement basic forensic procedures.

REF: 13-547

48. Capturing volatile information can best be performed by capturing the entire _____, which is a snapshot of the current state of the computer that contains all current settings and data.
    A. system image
    B. RAM
    C. cache
    D. network state
    Security+ SY0-401 Objective 2.4: Given a scenario, implement basic forensic procedures.
    REF: 13-547

49. During the process of _____, hashing algorithms are used as part of the validation process by mirror image backup programs to ensure accuracy.
    A. establishing a chain of custody
    B. preserving the evidence of a crime
    C. securing a crime scene
    D. examining the evidence
    Security+ SY0-401 Objective 2.4: Given a scenario, implement basic forensic procedures.
    REF: 13-547

50. While _____, any data such as contents of RAM, current network connections, logon sessions, network traffic and logs, and any open files must be captured and saved.
    A. establishing a chain of custody
    B. preserving the evidence of a crime
    C. securing a crime scene
    D. examining the evidence of a crime
    Security+ SY0-401 Objective 2.4: Given a scenario, implement basic forensic procedures.
    REF: 13-547

51. During which stage of forensic analysis might big data analysis be conducted?
    A. Establishing a chain of custody
    B. Preserving the evidence
    C. Securing a crime scene
    D. Examining the evidence
    Security+ SY0-401 Objective 2.4: Given a scenario, implement basic forensic procedures.
    REF: 13-548

2

52. A _____ includes the documentation of all the serial numbers of the systems involved, who handled and had custody of the systems and for what length of time, how the computer was shipped, and any other steps in the process.

    A. risk assessment

    B. tabletop exercise

    C. chain of custody

    D. succession plan

    Security+ SY0-401 Objective 2.4: Given a scenario, implement basic forensic procedures.

    REF: 13-548

53. The term _____ is used to describe a process of documentation that shows that the evidence was under strict control at all times and no unauthorized individuals were given the opportunity to corrupt the evidence.

    A. risk assessment

    B. tabletop exercise

    C. chain of custody

    D. succession plan

    Security+ SY0-401 Objective 2.4: Given a scenario, implement basic forensic procedures.

    REF: 13-548

54. Which incident procedure involves identifying the incident, notifying key personnel, and escalating procedures as necessary?

    A. Analysis

    B. Execution

    C. Preparation

    D. Prevention

    Security+ SY0-401 Objective 2.5: Summarize common incident response procedures.

    REF: 13-550

55. Which incident procedure takes damage and loss control steps to mitigate damage, particularly in the event of a data breach?

    A. Analysis

    B. Execution

    C. Preparation

    D. Prevention

    Security+ SY0-401 Objective 2.5: Summarize common incident response procedures.

    REF: 13-550

56. Which incident procedure involves isolating equipment by either quarantine or the entire removal of the device itself?

A. Analysis

B. Execution

C. Preparation

D. Prevention

Security+ SY0-401 Objective 2.5: Summarize common incident response procedures.

REF: 13-550

57. During which phase of incident response would you review the "lessons learned?"

A. Analysis

B. Execution

C. Preparation

D. Prevention

Security+ SY0-401 Objective 2.5: Summarize common incident response procedures.

REF: 13-550

58. When an event occurs, the computer forensics response team must be contacted immediately. This team serves as _____ whenever digital evidence needs to be preserved.

A. electronic EMTs

B. event coordinators

C. key personnel

D. first responders

Security+ SY0-401 Objective 2.5: Summarize common incident response procedures.

REF: 13-546

59. Which aspect of awareness and training involves instruction regarding the reasons why it is necessary to adhere to the organization's established security strategy?

A. Instruction on secure user practices

B. Compliance training

C. Raising awareness of threats introduced by technology

D. Instruction on social networking

Security+ SY0-401 Objective 2.6: Explain the importance of security-related awareness and training.

REF: 14-585

60. Which user practice, as part of an organization's security strategy, requires employees to clear their workspace of all papers at the end of each business day?

A. Password behaviors

B. Data handling

C. Clean desk policy

D. Portable data

Security+ SY0-401 Objective 2.6: Explain the importance of security-related awareness and training.

REF: 14-586

61. Which user practice, as part of an organization's security strategy, insists that all data temporarily stored on a laptop computer should be encrypted?

A. Password behaviors

B. Data handling

C. Clean desk policy

D. Portable data

Security+ SY0-401 Objective 2.6: Explain the importance of security-related awareness and training.

REF: 14-586

62. Which user practice eschews the idea of allowing another person to enter a secure area with you without displaying an ID card?

A. Prevent tailgating

B. Data handling

C. Clean desk policy

D. Portable data

Security+ SY0-401 Objective 2.6: Explain the importance of security-related awareness and training.

REF: 14-586

63. A _____ network does not have servers, so each device simultaneously functions as both a client and a server to all other devices connected to the network.

A. star

B. ring

C. client server

D. P2P

Security+ SY0-401 Objective 2.6: Explain the importance of security-related awareness and training.

REF: 14-586

64. The most common type of P2P network is known as _____.
    A. mesh
    B. ring
    C. BitTorrent
    D. star
    Security+ SY0-401 Objective 2.6: Explain the importance of security-related awareness and training.
    REF: 14-587

65. Grouping individuals and organizations into clusters or groups based on some sort of affiliation is called _____.
    A. star networking
    B. social networking
    C. profile networking
    D. peer to peer networking
    Security+ SY0-401 Objective 2.6: Explain the importance of security-related awareness and training.
    REF: 14-587

66. _____ involves specialized training that is customized to the specific role that an employee holds in the organization.
    A. Social networking
    B. Personnel identification
    C. User training
    D. Role-based training
    Security+ SY0-401 Objective 2.6: Explain the importance of security-related awareness and training.
    REF: 14-591

67. A _____ attempts to discourage security violations before they occur.
    A. preventive control
    B. compensating control
    C. detective control
    D. deterrent control
    Security+ SY0-401 Objective 2.7: Compare and contrast physical security and environmental controls.
    REF: 4-139

2

68. _____ work to prevent the threat from coming into contact with the vulnerability.
    A. Preventive controls
    B. Compensating controls
    C. Administrative controls
    D. Deterrent controls
    Security+ SY0-401 Objective 2.7: Compare and contrast physical security and environmental controls.
    REF: 4-139

69. _____ are the processes for developing and ensuring that policies and procedures are carried out.
    A. Preventive controls
    B. Compensating controls
    C. Administrative controls
    D. Deterrent controls
    Security+ SY0-401 Objective 2.7: Compare and contrast physical security and environmental controls.
    REF: 4-139

70. What type of controls are designed to identify any threat that has reached the system?
    A. Preventive controls
    B. Compensating controls
    C. Detective controls
    D. Deterrent controls
    Security+ SY0-401 Objective 2.7: Compare and contrast physical security and environmental controls.
    REF: 4-140

71. Which method would you use to extinguish a Class A fire?
    A. Foam, dry chemical, or carbon dioxide to put out the fire by smothering it or cutting off the oxygen
    B. Dry powder or other special sodium extinguishing agents
    C. Water, water-based chemical, foam, or multipurpose dry chemical
    D. Special extinguisher converts oils to noncombustible soaps
    Security+ SY0-401 Objective 2.7: Compare and contrast physical security and environmental controls.
    REF: 13-541

72. Which method would you use to extinguish a Class C fire?

    A. Foam, dry chemical, or carbon dioxide to put out the fire by smothering it or cutting off the oxygen

    B. Dry powder or other special sodium extinguishing agents

    C. Water, water-based chemical, foam, or multipurpose dry chemical

    D. Special extinguisher converts oils to noncombustible soaps

    Security+ SY0-401 Objective 2.7: Compare and contrast physical security and environmental controls.

    REF: 13-541

73. Which method would you use to extinguish a Class K fire?

    A. Foam, dry chemical, or carbon dioxide to put out the fire by smothering it or cutting off the oxygen

    B. Dry powder or other special sodium extinguishing agents

    C. Water, water-based chemical, foam, or multipurpose dry chemical

    D. Special extinguisher converts oils to noncombustible soaps

    Security+ SY0-401 Objective 2.7: Compare and contrast physical security and environmental controls.

    REF: 13-541

74. Which method would you use to extinguish a Class D fire?

    A. Foam, dry chemical, or carbon dioxide to put out the fire by smothering it or cutting off the oxygen

    B. Dry powder or other special sodium extinguishing agents

    C. Water, water-based chemical, foam, or multipurpose dry chemical

    D. Special extinguisher converts oils to noncombustible soaps

    Security+ SY0-401 Objective 2.7: Compare and contrast physical security and environmental controls.

    REF: 13-541

75. A defense for shielding an electromagnetic field is a _____, which is a metallic enclosure that prevents the entry or escape of an electromagnetic field.

    A. server cluster

    B. rollover server

    C. failsafe server

    D. Faraday cage

    Security+ SY0-401 Objective 2.7: Compare and contrast physical security and environmental controls.

    REF: 13-543

2

76. In a data center using a(n) _____ layout, the server racks are lined up in alternating rows, with cold air intakes facing one direction and hot air exhausts facing the other direction.

    A. RH+/RH-

    B. hot aisle/cold aisle

    C. class 1/class 2

    D. class A/class B

    Security+ SY0-401 Objective 2.7: Compare and contrast physical security and environmental controls.

    REF: 13-544

77. The term _____ is used to describe the sudden flow of electric current between two objects, which can destroy electronic equipment.

    A. electrostatic discharge

    B. HVAC

    C. RAID

    D. Faraday cage

    Security+ SY0-401 Objective 2.7: Compare and contrast physical security and environmental controls.

    REF: 13-544

78. _____ is usually a tall, permanent structure to keep out individuals for maintaining security.

    A. A guard

    B. A mantrap

    C. A barricade

    D. Fencing

    Security+ SY0-401 Objective 2.7: Compare and contrast physical security and environmental controls.

    REF: 4-140

79. Video surveillance uses video cameras to transmit a signal to a specific and limited set of receivers called _____.

    A. closed circuit television

    B. infrared sensors

    C. seismic sensors

    D. magnetic sensors

    Security+ SY0-401 Objective 2.7: Compare and contrast physical security and environmental controls.

    REF: 4-141

80. _____ are most often used for directing large crowds or restricting vehicular traffic and are generally not designed to keep out individuals.

A. Barricades

B. Proximity readers

C. Mantraps

D. Protected distribution systems

Security+ SY0-401 Objective 2.7: Compare and contrast physical security and environmental controls.

REF: 4-141

81. A _____ is a system of cable conduits used to protect classified information that is being transmitted between two secure areas.

A. barricade

B. protected distribution system

C. mantrap

D. proximity reader

Security+ SY0-401 Objective 2.7: Compare and contrast physical security and environmental controls.

REF: 4-146

82. _____ involves determining an object's change in position in relation to its surroundings.

A. Motion detection

B. Video surveillance

C. Software baselining

D. Patch management

Security+ SY0-401 Objective 2.7: Compare and contrast physical security and environmental controls.

REF: 4-142

83. A _____ lock extends a solid metal bar into the door frame for extra security.

A. deadbolt

B. keyed entry

C. store entry double cylinder

D. cipher lock

Security+ SY0-401 Objective 2.7: Compare and contrast physical security and environmental controls.

REF: 4-143

84. Which category of commercial door locks includes a keyed cylinder in both the outside and inside knobs so that a key in either knob locks or unlocks both at the same time?

    A. storeroom

    B. classroom

    C. store entry double cylinder

    D. communicating double cylinder

    Security+ SY0-401 Objective 2.7: Compare and contrast physical security and environmental controls.

    REF: 4-143

85. _____ are combination locks that use buttons that must be pushed in the proper sequence to open the door.

    A. Deadbolt locks

    B. Keyed entry locks

    C. Store entry double cylinder locks

    D. Cipher locks

    Security+ SY0-401 Objective 2.7: Compare and contrast physical security and environmental controls.

    REF: 4-144

86. A(n) _____ is designed to separate a nonsecured area from a secured area via a vestibule featuring two interlocking doors.

    A. proximity reader

    B. mantrap

    C. access list

    D. protected distribution system

    Security+ SY0-401 Objective 2.7: Compare and contrast physical security and environmental controls.

    REF: 4-146

87. A(n) _____ is a device that detects an emitted signal in order to identify the owner.

    A. protected distribution system

    B. mantrap

    C. proximity reader

    D. access list

    Security+ SY0-401 Objective 2.7: Compare and contrast physical security and environmental controls.

    REF: 4-145

88. A(n) _____ is a record or list of individuals who have permission to enter a secure area, along with the time they entered and the time they left the area.

    A. protected distribution system

    B. access list

    C. mantrap

    D. proximity reader

    Security+ SY0–401 Objective 2.7: Compare and contrast physical security and environmental controls.

    REF: 4-146

89. Standard _____ can use fingerprints or other unique characteristics of a person's face, hands, or eyes (irises and retinas) to authenticate a user.

    A. smart cards

    B. biometrics

    C. passwords

    D. tokens

    Security+ SY0–401 Objective 2.7: Compare and contrast physical security and environmental controls.

    REF: 12-495

90. _____ involves determining in advance who will be authorized to take over in the event of the incapacitation or death of key employees.

    A. Succession planning

    B. Business continuity planning

    C. Business impact analysis

    D. Risk analysis

    Security+ SY0–401 Objective 2.8: Summarize risk management best practices.

    REF: 13-525

91. _____ is the process of identifying exposure to threats, creating preventive and recovery procedures, and then testing them to determine if they are sufficient.

    A. Business continuity planning and testing

    B. Succession planning

    C. Risk analysis

    D. Business impact analysis

    Security+ SY0–401 Objective 2.8: Summarize risk management best practices.

    REF: 13-525

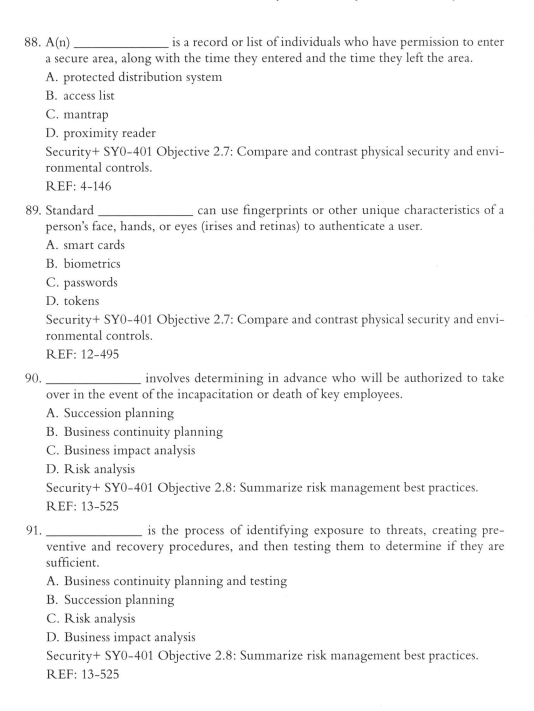

92. A _____ identifies mission-critical business functions and quantifies the impact a loss of such functions may have on the organization in terms of its operational and financial position.

    A. tabletop exercise

    B. succession analysis

    C. business impact analysis

    D. recovery analysis

    Security+ SY0-401 Objective 2.8: Summarize risk management best practices.

    REF: 13-526

93. A _____ typically begins by identifying threats through a risk assessment.

    A. business impact analysis

    B. tabletop exercise

    C. recovery analysis

    D. succession analysis

    Security+ SY0-401 Objective 2.8: Summarize risk management best practices.

    REF: 13-526

94. _____ involves developing an outline of procedures that are to be followed in the event of major IT incident (a denial-of-service attack) or an incident that directly impacts IT (a building fire).

    A. Risk assessment

    B. IT contingency planning

    C. Succession planning

    D. System recovery planning

    Security+ SY0-401 Objective 2.8: Summarize risk management best practices.

    REF: 13-526

95. _____ plans typically include procedures to address redundancy and fault tolerance as well as data backups.

    A. System recovery

    B. Succession

    C. Risk assessment

    D. Disaster recovery

    Security+ SY0-401 Objective 2.8: Summarize risk management best practices.

    REF: 13-526

96. _____ simulate(s) an emergency situation but in an informal and stress-free environment.
    A. Risk analysis
    B. Tabletop exercises
    C. IT contingency planning
    D. System recovery planning
    Security+ SY0-401 Objective 2.8: Summarize risk management best practices.
    REF: 13-529

97. The term _____ is used to describe a system that can function for an extended period of time with little downtime.
    A. reduced availability
    B. low availability
    C. high availability
    D. extended availability
    Security+ SY0-401 Objective 2.8: Summarize risk management best practices.
    REF: 13-529

98. The term _____ is used to describe a component or entity in a system which, if it no longer functions, would adversely affect the entire system.
    A. order of volatility
    B. Faraday cage
    C. downtime
    D. single point of failure
    Security+ SY0-401 Objective 2.8: Summarize risk management best practices.
    REF: 13-529

99. A _____ is the combination of two or more servers that are interconnected to appear as one.
    A. server cluster
    B. redundant server
    C. client cluster
    D. shared server
    Security+ SY0-401 Objective 2.8: Summarize risk management best practices.
    REF: 13-530

2

100. The term _____ is used to describe a technology that uses multiple hard disk drives for increased reliability and performance.

    A. Redundant Array of IDE Drives

    B. Redundant Array of Independent Drives

    C. Resistant Architecture of Inter-Related Data Storage

    D. Resilient Architecture for Interdependent Discs

    Security+ SY0-401 Objective 2.8: Summarize risk management best practices.

    REF: 13-531

101. Within networks, _____ can provide a degree of network redundancy by blocking traffic to servers that are not functioning.

    A. protocol analyzers

    B. routers

    C. load balancers

    D. switches

    Security+ SY0-401 Objective 2.8: Summarize risk management best practices.

    REF: 13-535

102. A _____ is generally run by a commercial disaster recovery service that allows a business to continue computer and network operations to maintain business continuity.

    A. warm site

    B. cold site

    C. hot site

    D. split-site

    Security+ SY0-401 Objective 2.8: Summarize risk management best practices.

    REF: 13-536

103. A _____ provides office space, but the customer must provide and install all the equipment needed to continue operations.

    A. warm site

    B. split site

    C. hot site

    D. cold site

    Security+ SY0-401 Objective 2.8: Summarize risk management best practices.

    REF: 13-536

104. A _____ has all the equipment installed but does not have active Internet or telecommunications facilities, and does not have current backups of data.

    A. warm site

    B. cold site

    C. hot site

    D. split–site

    Security+ SY0–401 Objective 2.8: Summarize risk management best practices.

    REF: 13-536

105. What two elements are used in the calculation to determine when data backups should be performed?

    A. Recovery point objective and least time objective

    B. Recovery time objective and least time objective

    C. Least time objective and average time objective

    D. Recovery point objective and recovery time objective

    Security+ SY0–401 Objective 2.8: Summarize risk management best practices.

    REF: 13-538

106. Which security goal utilizes encryption, steganography, and access controls as common controls?

    A. Safety

    B. Integrity

    C. Confidentiality

    D. Availability

    Security+ SY0–401 Objective 2.9: Given a scenario, select the appropriate control to meet the goals of security.

    REF: 15-626

107. Which security goal implements hashing, digital signatures, certificates, and non-repudiation tools as common controls?

    A. Safety

    B. Integrity

    C. Confidentiality

    D. Availability

    Security+ SY0–401 Objective 2.9: Given a scenario, select the appropriate control to meet the goals of security.

    REF: 15-626

108. Which security goal employs redundancy, fault tolerance, and patching as common controls?

    A. Safety

    B. Integrity

    C. Confidentiality

    D. Availability

    Security+ SY0-401 Objective 2.9: Given a scenario, select the appropriate control to meet the goals of security.

    REF: 15-626

109. Which security goal utilizes locks, CCTV, escape plans and routes, and safety drills as common controls?

    A. Safety

    B. Integrity

    C. Confidentiality

    D. Availability

    Security+ SY0-401 Objective 2.9: Given a scenario, select the appropriate control to meet the goals of security.

    REF: 15-626

110. When defending external perimeters, most _____ is/are accompanied with a sign that explains the area is restricted and proper lighting so the area can be viewed after dark.

    A. deadbolts

    B. keyed locks

    C. fencing

    D. cipher locks

    Security+ SY0-401 Objective 2.9: Given a scenario, select the appropriate control to meet the goals of security.

    REF: 4-140

3.0

THREATS AND VULNERABILITIES

TEST PREPARATION QUESTIONS

1. Which term describes software that enters a computer system without the user's knowledge or consent and then performs an unwanted and usually harmful action?

   A. Sniffer

   B. Phishing

   C. Malware

   D. Bloatware

   Security+ SY0-401 Objective 3.1: Explain types of malware.

   REF: 2-51

2. What type of mutating malware changes its internal code to one of a set number of predefined mutations whenever it is executed?

   A. Oligomorphic malware

   B. Polymorphic malware

   C. Metamorphic malware

   D. Circulation malware

   Security+ SY0-401 Objective 3.1: Explain types of malware.

   REF: 2-52

3. What type of malware can actually rewrite its own code and thus appears different each time it is executed?

   A. Circulation malware

   B. Metamorphic malware

   C. Oligomorphic malware

   D. Polymorphic malware

   Security+ SY0-401 Objective 3.1: Explain types of malware.

   REF: 2-52

4. The primary traits that malware possesses are circulation, infection, concealment, and _____.

   A. interruption

   B. injection

   C. mutation

   D. payload capabilities

   Security+ SY0–401 Objective 3.1: Explain types of malware.

   REF: 2-52

5. Which term describes malicious computer code that reproduces itself on the same computer?

   A. Worm

   B. Virus

   C. Adware

   D. Trojan

   Security+ SY0–401 Objective 3.1: Explain types of malware.

   REF: 2-53

6. What type of virus goes to great lengths to avoid detection?

   A. Worm

   B. Logic bomb

   C. Armored virus

   D. Trojan

   Security+ SY0–401 Objective 3.1: Explain types of malware.

   REF: 2-55

7. What term refers to a malicious program that uses a computer network to replicate?

   A. Trojan

   B. Virus

   C. Adware

   D. Worm

   Security+ SY0–401 Objective 3.1: Explain types of malware.

   REF: 2-57

8. Which type of malware is an executable program that masquerades as performing a benign activity but also does something malicious?

   A. Trojan

   B. Worm

   C. Backdoor

   D. Rootkit

   Security+ SY0–401 Objective 3.1: Explain types of malware.

   REF: 2-58

9. Which term describes a set of software tools used to hide the actions or presence of other types of software?

A. Bloatware

B. Adware

C. Rootkit

D. Trojan

Security+ SY0-401 Objective 3.1: Explain types of malware.

REF: 2-58

10. Which type of malware secretly spies on users by collecting information without their consent?

A. Spyware

B. Adware

C. Rootkit

D. Trojan

Security+ SY0-401 Objective 3.1: Explain types of malware.

REF: 2-60

11. Which type of malware delivers advertising content in a manner that is unexpected and unwanted by the user?

A. Armored virus

B. Ransomware

C. Spyware

D. Adware

Security+ SY0-401 Objective 3.1: Explain types of malware.

REF: 2-61

12. Which type of malware prevents a user's device from properly operating until a fee is paid?

A. Spyware

B. Ransomware

C. Logic bomb

D. Trojan

Security+ SY0-401 Objective 3.1: Explain types of malware.

REF: 2-62

13. Which term defines computer code that is typically added to a legitimate program but lies dormant until it is triggered by a specific logical event?

    A. Trojan

    B. Rootkit

    C. Ransomware

    D. Logic bomb

    Security+ SY0-401 Objective 3.1: Explain types of malware.

    REF: 2-64

14. When hundreds, thousands, or even hundreds of thousands of zombie computers are gathered into a logical computer network, they create a _____ under the control of the attacker.

    A. botnet

    B. DMZ

    C. proxy

    D. flock

    Security+ SY0-401 Objective 3.1: Explain types of malware.

    REF: 2-65

15. Which type of malware gives access to a computer, program, or service that circumvents any normal security protections?

    A. Trojan

    B. Logic bomb

    C. Backdoor

    D. Spyware

    Security+ SY0-401 Objective 3.1: Explain types of malware.

    REF: 2-65

16. What type of attack sends an email or displays a web announcement that falsely claims to be from a legitimate enterprise in an attempt to trick the user into surrendering private information?

    A. Spoofing

    B. Phishing

    C. Spim

    D. Spam

    Security+ SY0-401 Objective 3.2: Summarize various types of attacks.

    REF: 2-68

17. Whereas phishing involves sending millions of generic email messages to users, _____ targets only specific users.

    A. spear phishing

    B. whaling

    C. vishing

    D. spim

    Security+ SY0-401 Objective 3.2: Summarize various types of attacks.

    REF: 2-70

18. In which type of attack can a telephone call be used instead of email to contact the potential victim?

    A. Whaling

    B. Vishing

    C. Spim

    D. Pharming

    Security+ SY0-401 Objective 3.2: Summarize various types of attacks.

    REF: 2-70

19. Which phishing attack variation automatically redirects the user to a fake site?

    A. Whaling

    B. Vishing

    C. Pharming

    D. Spear phishing

    Security+ SY0-401 Objective 3.2: Summarize various types of attacks.

    REF: 2-70

20. Which variation of spam uses graphical images of text in order to circumvent basic filters?

    A. Hoax spam

    B. Web spam

    C. Image spam

    D. HTML spam

    Security+ SY0-401 Objective 3.2: Summarize various types of attacks.

    REF: 2-71

3

21. Which attack exploits typing errors made by users when entering a uniform resource locator (URL) address or domain name?

    A. Watering hole

    B. Typo squatting

    C. Hoaxes

    D. Spim

    Security+ SY0-401 Objective 3.2: Summarize various types of attacks.

    REF: 2-72

22. Which attack consists of a deliberate attempt to prevent authorized users from accessing a system by overwhelming that system with requests?

    A. Denial of service

    B. Spim

    C. Privilege escalation

    D. Transitive access

    Security+ SY0-401 Objective 3.2: Summarize various types of attacks.

    REF: 3-109

23. In what attack does an attacker broadcast a ping request to all computers on the network but changes the address from which the request came to the victim's computer?

    A. SYN flood

    B. Ping flood

    C. Ping of death

    D. Smurf attack

    Security+ SY0-401 Objective 3.2: Summarize various types of attacks.

    REF: 3-110

24. Which term describes the impersonation of another computer or device?

    A. DDoS

    B. DoS

    C. Transitive access

    D. Spoofing

    Security+ SY0-401 Objective 3.2: Summarize various types of attacks.

    REF: 3-110

25. Which attack makes it appear that two computers are communicating with each other, when actually they are sending and receiving data with a computer between them?

    A. Spoof

    B. Man-in-the-middle

    C. DoS

    D. Transitive access

    Security+ SY0-401 Objective 3.2: Summarize various types of attacks.

    REF: 3-112

26. Which attack makes a copy of an intercepted transmission before sending it to the recipient to be used at a later time?

    A. Replay

    B. Man-in-the-middle

    C. Transitive access

    D. Spoof

    Security+ SY0-401 Objective 3.2: Summarize various types of attacks.

    REF: 3-112

27. An attacker can modify the MAC address in the ARP cache so that the corresponding IP address points to a different computer. This is known as _____.

    A. network poisoning

    B. cache poisoning

    C. DNS poisoning

    D. ARP poisoning

    Security+ SY0-401 Objective 3.2: Summarize various types of attacks.

    REF: 3-113

28. What is the term for exploiting a vulnerability in software to gain access to resources that the user normally would be restricted from accessing?

    A. Rootkit

    B. Spim

    C. Privilege escalation

    D. Transitive access

    Security+ SY0-401 Objective 3.2: Summarize various types of attacks.

    REF: 3-117

3

29. Which password attack tries every possible combination of letters, numbers, and characters to create candidates?

    A. Pattern

    B. Hybrid

    C. Dictionary

    D. Brute force

    Security+ SY0-401 Objective 3.2: Summarize various types of attacks.

    REF: 12-484

30. Which password attack begins with the attacker creating digests of common words as candidates and then comparing them against those in a stolen digest file?

    A. Brute force

    B. Dictionary

    C. Pattern

    D. Hybrid

    Security+ SY0-401 Objective 3.2: Summarize various types of attacks.

    REF: 12-485

31. What term defines a compressed representation of cleartext passwords that are related and organized in a sequence?

    A. Pattern dictionary

    B. Hybrid dictionary

    C. Rainbow table

    D. Pattern table

    Security+ SY0-401 Objective 3.2: Summarize various types of attacks.

    REF: 12-486

32. What term describes a means of gathering information for an attack by relying on the weaknesses of individuals?

    A. Social engineering

    B. Spoofing

    C. Phishing

    D. Identity theft

    Security+ SY0-401 Objective 3.3: Summarize social engineering attacks and the associated effectiveness with each attack.

    REF: 2-67

33. "I'm the CEO calling" is an example of the _____ principle applied in a social engineering attack.

    A. Intimidation

    B. Authority

    C. Urgency

    D. Trust

    Security+ SY0-401 Objective 3.3: Summarize social engineering attacks and the associated effectiveness with each attack.

    REF: 2-67

34. A social engineering attack of the form "if you don't reset my password, I will call your supervisor" relies on what principle?

    A. urgency

    B. intimidation

    C. authority

    D. trust

    Security+ SY0-401 Objective 3.3: Summarize social engineering attacks and the associated effectiveness with each attack.

    REF: 2-67

35. "I called last week and your colleague reset my password" is an example of a social engineering attack based on what principle?

    A. Consensus/social proof

    B. Authority

    C. Repetition

    D. Familiarity

    Security+ SY0-401 Objective 3.3: Summarize social engineering attacks and the associated effectiveness with each attack.

    REF: 2-67

36. "I can't waste time here" is a social engineering attack based on the _____ principle.

    A. intimidation

    B. social proof

    C. urgency

    D. scarcity

    Security+ SY0-401 Objective 3.3: Summarize social engineering attacks and the associated effectiveness with each attack.

    REF: 2-67

3

37. A social engineering attack of the form "My meeting with the board starts in five minutes" relies on what principle?

    A. Intimidation

    B. Authority

    C. Urgency

    D. Scarcity

    Security+ SY0-401 Objective 3.3: Summarize social engineering attacks and the associated effectiveness with each attack.

    REF: 2-67

38. "I remember reading a good evaluation on you" is an example of a social engineering attack based on what principle?

    A. Social proof

    B. Consensus

    C. Familiarity/liking

    D. Trust

    Security+ SY0-401 Objective 3.3: Summarize social engineering attacks and the associated effectiveness with each attack.

    REF: 2-67

39. "You know who I am" is an attack is based on the _____ principle.

    A. Familiarity/liking

    B. Intimidation

    C. Authority

    D. Trust

    Security+ SY0-401 Objective 3.3: Summarize social engineering attacks and the associated effectiveness with each attack.

    REF: 2-67

40. What type of attack is characterized by the attacker masquerading as a real or fictitious character and then playing out the role of that person on a victim?

    A. Impersonation

    B. Phishing

    C. Vishing

    D. Tailgating

    Security+ SY0-401 Objective 3.3: Summarize social engineering attacks and the associated effectiveness with each attack.

    REF: 2-68

41. Which type of phishing attack targets wealthy individuals or senior executives within a business?

    A. Spim

    B. Hoaxes

    C. Whaling

    D. Spear phishing

    Security+ SY0-401 Objective 3.3: Summarize social engineering attacks and the associated effectiveness with each attack.

    REF: 2-70

42. Which term refers to a false warning, often contained in an email message claiming to come from the IT department?

    A. Hoax

    B. Spim

    C. Whaling

    D. Spear phishing

    Security+ SY0-401 Objective 3.3: Summarize social engineering attacks and the associated effectiveness with each attack.

    REF: 2-72

43. Which attack involves digging through trash receptacles to find information that can be useful in an attack?

    A. Office cleaning

    B. Piggybacking

    C. Dumpster diving

    D. Tailgating

    Security+ SY0-401 Objective 3.3: Summarize social engineering attacks and the associated effectiveness with each attack.

    REF: 2-73

44. Once an authorized person opens a secured door, virtually any number of individuals can follow behind and also enter. This is known as _____.

    A. a man trap

    B. door surfing

    C. shoulder surfing

    D. tailgating

    Security+ SY0-401 Objective 3.3: Summarize social engineering attacks and the associated effectiveness with each attack.

    REF: 2-73

3

45. What term describes someone who "casually observes" someone entering an authorized code on a keypad?

    A. Shoulder surfing

    B. Tailgating

    C. Piggybacking

    D. Code riding

    Security+ SY0-401 Objective 3.3: Summarize social engineering attacks and the associated effectiveness with each attack.

    REF: 2-74

46. If an attacker manages to connect to the enterprise wired network through a(n) _____, she also could read broadcast and multicast wired network traffic that leaks from the wired network to the wireless network.

    A. evil twin

    B. packet sniffer

    C. rogue access point

    D. replay attack

    Security+ SY0-401 Objective 3.4: Explain types of wireless attacks.

    REF: 9-370

47. Radio Frequency (RF) _____ is a type of wireless DoS attack in which the attacker intentionally floods the RF spectrum with extraneous RF signal "noise" that creates interference and prevents communications from occurring.

    A. jacking

    B. sniffing

    C. chalking

    D. jamming

    Security+ SY0-401 Objective 3.4: Explain types of wireless attacks.

    REF: 9-373

48. A(n) _____ is an access point (AP) set up by an attacker, designed to mimic an authorized AP.

    A. rogue access point

    B. evil twin

    C. packet sniffer

    D. SoftAP

    Security+ SY0-401 Objective 3.4: Explain types of wireless attacks.

    REF: 9-370

49. An attacker can search for wireless signals from an automobile or on foot using a portable computing device. This is known as _____.

   A. bluejacking

   B. bluesnarfing

   C. war chalking

   D. war driving

   Security+ SY0-401 Objective 3.4: Explain types of wireless attacks.

   REF: 9-375

50. What is the name of the wireless attack in which an attacker sends unsolicited messages to Bluetooth-enabled devices?

   A. Bluejacking

   B. Bluesnarfing

   C. Bluechalking

   D. Smurf attack

   Security+ SY0-401 Objective 3.4: Explain types of wireless attacks.

   REF: 9-364

51. What is the name of the wireless attack in which the attacker copies emails, calendars, contact lists, cell phone pictures, or videos by connecting to the Bluetooth device without the owner's knowledge or permission?

   A. Bluejacking

   B. Bluesnarfing

   C. Bluechalking

   D. Smurf attack

   Security+ SY0-401 Objective 3.4: Explain types of wireless attacks.

   REF: 9-364

52. What is the process of documenting and then advertising the location of wireless LANs for others to use?

   A. War chalking

   B. Fencing

   C. Tailgating

   D. Dumpster diving

   Security+ SY0-401 Objective 3.4: Explain types of wireless attacks.

   REF: 9-375

3

53. Which security vulnerability applies to WEP's initialization vector (IV)?
    A. Turning off its broadcast may prevent users from being able to freely roam from one AP coverage area to another.
    B. Its short length limits its strength.
    C. Its last character is only a checksum.
    D. It is exchanged between wireless devices and the access point (AP) in an unencrypted format.
    Security+ SY0-401 Objective 3.4: Explain types of wireless attacks.
    REF: 9-376

54. Which wireless attack consists of picking up the radio frequency (RF) signal from an open or misconfigured access point and reading confidential wireless transmissions?
    A. Packet sniffing
    B. War driving
    C. Jamming
    D. Vishing
    Security+ SY0-401 Objective 3.4: Explain types of wireless attacks.
    REF: 9-370

55. Which near field communication (NFC) attack is performed by intercepting the NFC communications between devices and forging fictitious responses?
    A. Eavesdropping
    B. Data manipulation
    C. Device theft
    D. Man-in-the-middle
    Security+ SY0-401 Objective 3.4: Explain types of wireless attacks.
    REF: 9-366

56. What type of wireless attack is carried out by capturing the data being transmitted, recording it, and then sending it on to the original recipient without the attacker's presence being detected?
    A. Active man-in-the-middle attack
    B. Wireless replay attack
    C. Packet sniffing
    D. Rogue access point attack
    Security+ SY0-401 Objective 3.4: Explain types of wireless attacks.
    REF: 9-372

57. Which encryption technology functions as a "wrapper" around WEP by adding an additional layer of security but still preserving WEP's basic functionality?

    A. Challenge-Handshake Authentication Protocol (CHAP)

    B. Counter Mode with Cipher Block Chaining Message Authentication Code Protocol (CCMP)

    C. Password Authentication Protocol (PAP)

    D. Temporal Key Integrity Protocol (TKIP)

    Security+ SY0-401 Objective 3.4: Explain types of wireless attacks.

    REF: 9-380

58. Which security flaw applies to WPS using the Personal Identification Number (PIN) method?

    A. Turning off its broadcast may prevent users from being able to freely roam from one AP coverage area to another.

    B. Its short length limits its strength.

    C. Its last character is only a checksum.

    D. It is exchanged between wireless devices and the access point (AP) in an unencrypted format.

    Security+ SY0-401 Objective 3.4: Explain types of wireless attacks.

    REF: 9-377

59. In a wireless LAN (WLAN), turning off the _____ broadcast may prevent users from being able to freely roam from one AP coverage area to another.

    A. MAC address

    B. Service Set Identifier (SSID)

    C. WPS Personal Identification Number (PIN)

    D. WEP initialization vector (IV)

    Security+ SY0-401 Objective 3.4: Explain types of wireless attacks.

    REF: 9-379

60. An attacker using a protocol analyzer can easily see the _____ of an approved device and then substitute it on her own device.

    A. MAC address

    B. Service Set Identifier (SSID)

    C. WPS Personal Identification Number (PIN)

    D. WEP initialization vector (IV)

    Security+ SY0-401 Objective 3.4: Explain types of wireless attacks.

    REF: 9-378

3

61. A(n) _____ attack injects scripts into a web application server to direct attacks at unsuspecting clients, taking advantage of web applications that accept user input without validating it and use that input in a response.

    A. cross-site scripting (XSS)

    B. SQL injection

    C. XML injection

    D. flash cookie

    Security+ SY0-401 Objective 3.5: Explain types of application attacks.

    REF: 3-95

62. What type of attack targets database servers by introducing malicious commands into them, allowing the attacker to extract or manipulate information from the database?

    A. Phishing

    B. Header manipulation

    C. Cross-site scripting (XSS)

    D. SQL injection

    Security+ SY0-401 Objective 3.5: Explain types of application attacks.

    REF: 3-99

63. Which attack attempts to exploit the XML Path Language (XPath) queries that are built from user input?

    A. Cross-site scripting (XSS)

    B. Structured Query Language (SQL) injection

    C. DNS poisoning

    D. XPath injection

    Security+ SY0-401 Objective 3.5: Explain types of application attacks.

    REF: 3-100

64. A directory traversal uses _____ or takes advantage of a vulnerability to move from the root directory to restricted directories.

    A. root access

    B. malformed input

    C. SQL injection

    D. XML injection

    Security+ SY0-401 Objective 3.5: Explain types of application attacks.

    REF: 3-100

65. Which type of attack occurs when data overflows into the adjacent memory locations allowing an attacker to insert a new address pointing to the attacker's malware code?

    A. Address insertion

    B. Command injection

    C. Buffer overflow

    D. Integer overflow

    Security+ SY0-401 Objective 3.5: Explain types of application attacks.

    REF: 3-107

66. Which type of attack can be used to create a buffer overflow situation?

    A. Phishing attacks

    B. War driving

    C. Command injection

    D. Integer overflow attack

    Security+ SY0-401 Objective 3.5: Explain types of application attacks.

    REF: 3-108

67. Which type of attack exploits previously unknown vulnerabilities?

    A. Zero-day attack

    B. Smurf attack

    C. Tailgating

    D. Birthday attack

    Security+ SY0-401 Objective 3.5: Explain types of application attacks.

    REF: 3-95

68. Which type of cookie can be stolen and used to impersonate the user?

    A. Session cookie

    B. Flash cookie

    C. First-party cookie

    D. Third-party cookie

    Security+ SY0-401 Objective 3.5: Explain types of application attacks.

    REF: 3-104

69. Malicious _____ are commonly used to spread viruses, Trojans, and other malware when they are opened.

    A. cookies

    B. headers

    C. attachments

    D. logs

    Security+ SY0-401 Objective 3.5: Explain types of application attacks.

    REF: 3-105

3

70. Which type of cookie is significantly different from regular cookies in that it can store data more complex than the simple text that is typically found in a regular cookie?

    A. First-party cookie

    B. Third-party cookie

    C. Session cookie

    D. Flash cookie

    Security+ SY0-401 Objective 3.5: Explain types of application attacks.

    REF: 3-104

71. The defense against _____ attacks is to examine all user input before processing.

    A. ActiveX

    B. Zero day

    C. Header manipulation

    D. LDAP injection

    Security+ SY0-401 Objective 3.5: Explain types of application attacks.

    REF: 11-462

72. Attackers can take advantage of vulnerabilities in Microsoft's _____ to create malicious browser add-ons.

    A. Flash

    B. ActiveX

    C. cross-site scripting (XSS)

    D. locally shared objects (LSO)

    Security+ SY0-401 Objective 3.5: Explain types of application attacks.

    REF: 3-106

73. Which attack consists of impersonating the user by using her session token?

    A. Session hijacking

    B. Spoofing

    C. Man-in-the-middle attack

    D. Privilege escalation

    Security+ SY0-401 Objective 3.5: Explain types of application attacks.

    REF: 3-105

74. By inserting a(n) _____ in an HTTP header, an attacker can gain control of the remaining HTTP headers and body of the response.

    A. carriage return and line feed character (CRLF)

    B. checksum

    C. locally shared object (LSO)

    D. persistent cookie

    Security+ SY0–401 Objective 3.5: Explain types of application attacks.

    REF: 3-103

75. Which technique is often used in an arbitrary/remote code execution attack?

    A. HTTP header manipulation

    B. Heap spray

    C. SQL injection

    D. War driving

    Security+ SY0–401 Objective 3.5: Explain types of application attacks.

    REF: 3-109

76. When securing the operating system software, what should be done after developing the security policy?

    A. Configure the operating system security settings

    B. Establish a security baseline for the host

    C. Deploy and manage the security settings

    D. Implement an automated patch update service

    Security+ SY0–401 Objective 3.6: Analyze a scenario and select the appropriate type of mitigation and deterrent techniques.

    REF: 4-149

77. A typical configuration baseline includes changing any default settings that are insecure, _____, and enabling system security features (such as turning on the firewall).

    A. creating a security template

    B. implementing an automated patch update service

    C. eliminating any unnecessary software

    D. setting up the intrusion detection system alarms

    Security+ SY0–401 Objective 3.6: Analyze a scenario and select the appropriate type of mitigation and deterrent techniques.

    REF: 4-150

3

78. What OS hardening technique consists of removing all unnecessary features that may compromise an operating system?

    A. Kernel pruning

    B. Least privilege

    C. Reduce capabilities

    D. Read-only file system

    Security+ SY0-401 Objective 3.6: Analyze a scenario and select the appropriate type of mitigation and deterrent techniques.

    REF: 4-153

79. What is an appropriate defense mechanism against MAC flooding?

    A. Configure the switch so that only one port can be assigned per MAC address.

    B. Secure the switch in a locked room.

    C. Keep network connections secure by restricting physical access.

    D. Use a switch that can close ports with too many MAC addresses.

    Security+ SY0-401 Objective 3.6: Analyze a scenario and select the appropriate type of mitigation and deterrent techniques.

    REF: 7-276

80. Which IDS monitoring methodology should be used to catch application attempts to scan ports?

    A. Anomaly-based monitoring

    B. Signature-based monitoring

    C. Behavior-based monitoring

    D. Heuristic monitoring

    Security+ SY0-401 Objective 3.6: Analyze a scenario and select the appropriate type of mitigation and deterrent techniques.

    REF: 7-287

81. Which device log can be analyzed to find source-routed packets?

    A. Web server

    B. DHCP server

    C. Domain Name System (DNS)

    D. Firewall

    Security+ SY0-401 Objective 3.6: Analyze a scenario and select the appropriate type of mitigation and deterrent techniques.

    REF: 8-328

82. Which port security technique should be used to prevent an attacker from connecting to unused ports to access the network?

    A. Disabling unused interfaces

    B. MAC limiting

    C. MAC filtering

    D. Implementing IEEE 802.1x

    Security+ SY0-401 Objective 3.6: Analyze a scenario and select the appropriate type of mitigation and deterrent techniques.

    REF: 8-332

83. Which port security technique should be used to prevent unauthenticated devices from accessing the network?

    A. Disabling unused interfaces

    B. MAC limiting

    C. MAC filtering

    A. Implementing IEEE 802.1x

    Security+ SY0-401 Objective 3.6: Analyze a scenario and select the appropriate type of mitigation and deterrent techniques.

    REF: 8-333

84. How can a closed circuit television (CCTV) be used as a preventive control?

    A. By having a guard actively monitor the CCTV

    B. By using motion-tracking techniques

    C. By recording the video captured by the CCTV

    D. By examining a CCTV recording after a security event occurs

    Security+ SY0-401 Objective 3.6: Analyze a scenario and select the appropriate type of mitigation and deterrent techniques.

    REF: 4-141

85. Which tool used during threat modeling helps determine the threats that could pose a risk to assets?

    A. Honeypot

    B. Vulnerability scanner

    C. Baseline reporting

    D. Attack tree

    Security+ SY0-401 Objective 3.6: Analyze a scenario and select the appropriate type of mitigation and deterrent techniques.

    REF: 15-608

3

86. What is the name of the process that takes a snapshot of the current security of the organization?

    A. Assessment inventory

    B. Vulnerability appraisal

    C. Risk assessment

    D. Risk mitigation

    Security+ SY0-401 Objective 3.6: Analyze a scenario and select the appropriate type of mitigation and deterrent techniques.

    REF: 15-610

87. Which common control can be used to meet confidentiality security goals?

    A. Hashing

    B. Encryption

    C. Digital signatures

    D. Digital certificates

    Security+ SY0-401 Objective 3.6: Analyze a scenario and select the appropriate type of mitigation and deterrent techniques.

    REF: 15-626

88. What type of controls should be used to secure devices in scenarios where safety takes precedence over security?

    A. Fail-safe

    B. Fail-open

    C. Fail-secure

    D. Fail-lock

    Security+ SY0-401 Objective 3.6: Analyze a scenario and select the appropriate type of mitigation and deterrent techniques.

    REF: 15-627

89. Which action is considered a hardening technique?

    A. Disabling any unnecessary accounts

    B. Setting up IDS alerts

    C. Continuous security monitoring

    D. Establishing a remediation plan

    Security+ SY0-401 Objective 3.6: Analyze a scenario and select the appropriate type of mitigation and deterrent techniques.

    REF: 15-627

90. Which technique results from a sound and workable strategy toward managing risks?

    A. Selecting and configuring controls

    B. Hardening

    C. Security posture

    D. Reporting

    Security+ SY0-401 Objective 3.6: Analyze a scenario and select the appropriate type of mitigation and deterrent techniques.

    REF: 15-626

91. Which software tool can be used to search a system for port vulnerabilities?

    A. IPS

    B. Firewall

    C. Network sniffer

    D. Port scanner

    Security+ SY0-401 Objective 3.7: Given a scenario, use appropriate tools and techniques to discover security threats and vulnerabilities.

    REF: 15-615

92. Which is an example of a port scanner tool?

    A. Wireshark

    B. RADMIN

    C. Snort

    D. Bro

    Security+ SY0-401 Objective 3.7: Given a scenario, use appropriate tools and techniques to discover security threats and vulnerabilities.

    REF: 15-615

93. Which tool could be used to perform an inventory on the services and systems operating on a server by collecting the welcome message presented by a service when other programs connect to it?

    A. Sniffer

    B. Port scanner

    C. Banner grabbing

    D. IDS

    Security+ SY0-401 Objective 3.7: Given a scenario, use appropriate tools and techniques to discover security threats and vulnerabilities.

    REF: 15-616

3

94. Which term refers to hardware or software that captures packets to decode and analyze their contents?

    A. Network sniffer

    B. Protocol analyzer

    C. Port scanner

    D. Banner grabbing

    Security+ SY0-401 Objective 3.7: Given a scenario, use appropriate tools and techniques to discover security threats and vulnerabilities.

    REF: 15-617

95. Which tool can assist in network troubleshooting by detecting and diagnosing network problems such as addressing errors and protocol configuration mistakes?

    A. Port scanner

    B. Banner grabbing

    C. Network sniffer

    D. Protocol analyzer

    Security+ SY0-401 Objective 3.7: Given a scenario, use appropriate tools and techniques to discover security threats and vulnerabilities.

    REF: 15-617

96. Which type of tool has the capabilities to alert when new systems are added to the network, detect when an internal system begins to port scan other systems, and track all client and server application vulnerabilities?

    A. Vulnerability scanner

    B. Network sniffer

    C. Protocol analyzer

    D. Port scanner

    Security+ SY0-401 Objective 3.7: Given a scenario, use appropriate tools and techniques to discover security threats and vulnerabilities.

    REF: 15-619

97. Which standard was designed to promote open and publicly available security content?

    A. Hypertext Markup Language (HTML)

    B. Structured Query Language (SQL)

    C. Open Vulnerability and Assessment Language (OVAL)

    D. Extensible Markup Language (XML)

    Security+ SY0-401 Objective 3.7: Given a scenario, use appropriate tools and techniques to discover security threats and vulnerabilities.

    REF: 15-620

98. Which term refers to a computer typically located in an area with limited security and loaded with software and data files that appear to be authentic, but are actually imitations of real data files?

    A. Honeypot

    B. Honeynet

    C. Honeyhole

    D. DMZ

    Security+ SY0-401 Objective 3.7: Given a scenario, use appropriate tools and techniques to discover security threats and vulnerabilities.

    REF: 15-620

99. Which term refers to a network that is set up with intentional vulnerabilities?

    A. Honeypot

    B. Honeynet

    C. Botnet

    D. Honeyzone

    Security+ SY0-401 Objective 3.7: Given a scenario, use appropriate tools and techniques to discover security threats and vulnerabilities.

    REF: 15-621

100. What process allows you to better understand who the attackers are, why they attack, and what types of attacks might occur?

    A. Asset appraisal

    B. Vulnerability evaluation

    C. Asset identification

    D. Threat modeling

    Security+ SY0-401 Objective 3.7: Given a scenario, use appropriate tools and techniques to discover security threats and vulnerabilities.

    REF: 15-608

101. A(n) _____ provides a visual image of the attacks that could occur against an asset.

    A. attack tree

    B. asset model

    C. vulnerability map

    D. threat map

    Security+ SY0-401 Objective 3.7: Given a scenario, use appropriate tools and techniques to discover security threats and vulnerabilities.

    REF: 15-608

102. Which process involves determining the damage that would result from an attack and the likelihood that the vulnerability is a risk to the organization?

A. Risk assessment

B. Vulnerability appraisal

C. Threat modeling

D. Asset appraisal

Security+ SY0-401 Objective 3.7: Given a scenario, use appropriate tools and techniques to discover security threats and vulnerabilities.

REF: 15-611

103. Which term describes the process of defining a collection of hardware and software components along with their interfaces in order to create the framework for software development?

A. Design review

B. Architectural design review

C. Code review

D. Software review

Security+ SY0-401 Objective 3.7: Given a scenario, use appropriate tools and techniques to discover security threats and vulnerabilities.

REF: 15-613

104. While the code is being written in the context of software development, it is analyzed by a(n) _____ to assess its security.

A. design review

B. code review

C. architectural design review

D. verification review

Security+ SY0-401 Objective 3.7: Given a scenario, use appropriate tools and techniques to discover security threats and vulnerabilities.

REF: 15-613

105. What term refers to software development code that can be executed by unauthorized users?

A. Functionality description

B. Design surface

C. Code exposure

D. Attack surface

Security+ SY0-401 Objective 3.7: Given a scenario, use appropriate tools and techniques to discover security threats and vulnerabilities.

REF: 15-613

106. Which term refers to an automated software search through a system for any known security weaknesses that creates a report of those potential exposures?

    A. Port scanning

    B. Penetration testing

    C. Vulnerability scan

    D. Network testing

    Security+ SY0-401 Objective 3.8: Explain the proper use of penetration testing versus vulnerability scanning.

    REF: 15-621

107. Which type of scanning method involves a vulnerability scanner?

    A. Disruptive scanning

    B. Remote scanning

    C. Active scanning

    D. Passive scanning

    Security+ SY0-401 Objective 3.8: Explain the proper use of penetration testing versus vulnerability scanning.

    REF: 15-621

3

108. Vulnerability scans are usually performed from _____.

    A. inside the network DMZ

    B. outside the security perimeter

    C. inside the security perimeter

    D. outside the network DMZ

    Security+ SY0-401 Objective 3.8: Explain the proper use of penetration testing versus vulnerability scanning.

    REF: 15-621

109. Which vulnerability scan type attempts to actually penetrate the system in order to perform a simulated attack?

    A. Destructive

    B. Intrusive

    C. Full-scale

    D. Disruptive

    Security+ SY0-401 Objective 3.8: Explain the proper use of penetration testing versus vulnerability scanning.

    REF: 15-622

110. Which vulnerability scan type uses only available information to hypothesize the status of the vulnerability?

    A. Non-intrusive

    B. Passive

    C. Internal

    D. Virtual

    Security+ SY0-401 Objective 3.8: Explain the proper use of penetration testing versus vulnerability scanning.

    REF: 15-622

111. Which vulnerability scan type permits the username and password of an active account to be stored and used by the scanner, which allows the scanner to test for additional internal vulnerabilities?

    A. Active

    B. Intrusive

    C. Sanitized

    D. Credentialed

    Security+ SY0-401 Objective 3.8: Explain the proper use of penetration testing versus vulnerability scanning.

    REF: 15-622

112. Which vulnerability assessment procedure is designed to actually exploit any weaknesses in systems that are vulnerable?

    A. Threat testing

    B. Active vulnerability scanning

    C. Penetration testing

    D. Network probing

    Security+ SY0-401 Objective 3.8: Explain the proper use of penetration testing versus vulnerability scanning.

    REF: 15-622

113. Instead of using automated software, _____ relies upon the skill, knowledge, and cunning of the tester.

    A. penetration testing

    B. vulnerability scanning

    C. network probing

    D. network monitoring

    Security+ SY0-401 Objective 3.8: Explain the proper use of penetration testing versus vulnerability scanning.

    REF: 15-622

114. An "ethical hacker" is also known as a _____.

    A. white box hacker

    B. passive hacker

    C. white hat hacker

    D. hired hacker

    Security+ SY0-401 Objective 3.8: Explain the proper use of penetration testing versus vulnerability scanning.

    REF: 15-622

115. The goals of a _____ are to actively test all security controls and, when possible, bypass those controls, verify that a threat exists, and exploit any vulnerabilities.

    A. vulnerability scan

    B. penetration test

    C. credentialed vulnerability test

    D. threat scan

    Security+ SY0-401 Objective 3.8: Explain the proper use of penetration testing versus vulnerability scanning.

    REF: 15-623

116. Whereas _____ software may uncover a vulnerability, it provides no indication regarding the risk to that specific organization.

    A. network monitoring

    B. penetration test

    C. threat scan

    D. vulnerability scan

    Security+ SY0-401 Objective 3.8: Explain the proper use of penetration testing versus vulnerability scanning.

    REF: 15-623

117. In which scenario does the tester have no prior knowledge of the network infrastructure that is being tested?

    A. White box test

    B. Black box test

    C. Gray box test

    D. Beat box test

    Security+ SY0-401 Objective 3.8: Explain the proper use of penetration testing versus vulnerability scanning.

    REF: 15-623

3

118. Which test is the opposite of a black box test?

    A. Gray box

    B. Open box

    C. Transparent box

    D. White box

    Security+ SY0-401 Objective 3.8: Explain the proper use of penetration testing versus vulnerability scanning.

    REF: 15-623

119. With which type of test does the tester have an in-depth knowledge of the network and systems being tested, including network diagrams, IP addresses, and even the source code of custom applications?

    A. Black box

    B. Open box

    C. White box

    D. Gray box

    Security+ SY0-401 Objective 3.8: Explain the proper use of penetration testing versus vulnerability scanning.

    REF: 15-623

120. Which test provides some limited information to the tester?

    A. Gray box

    B. White box

    C. Black box

    D. Orange box

    Security+ SY0-401 Objective 3.8: Explain the proper use of penetration testing versus vulnerability scanning.

    REF: 15-623

4.0

Application, Data, and Host Security

Test Preparation Questions

1. Which term describes a software testing technique that deliberately provides invalid, unexpected, or random data as inputs to a computer program?

   A. Fuzzing

   B. Application hardening

   C. Cross-site scripting

   D. Black box testing

   Security+ SY0-401 Objective 4.1: Explain the importance of application security controls and techniques.

   REF: 4-159

2. An important step in developing secure applications is to account for _____, which are faults in a program that occur while the application is running.

   A. code omissions

   B. unnecessary redundancy

   C. integrity errors

   D. exceptions

   Security+ SY0-401 Objective 4.1: Explain the importance of application security controls and techniques.

   REF: 4-159

3. _____ refers to error handling that verifies responses the user makes to the application.

A. Baselining

B. Cross site scripting (XSS)

C. Output validation

D. Input validation

Security+ SY0-401 Objective 4.1: Explain the importance of application security controls and techniques.

REF: 4-159

4. _____ is the cause of several types of attacks such as cross-site scripting (XSS), SQL injection, and XML injection.

A. improper verification

B. output validation

C. application whitelisting

D. geo-tagging

Security+ SY0-401 Objective 4.1: Explain the importance of application security controls and techniques.

REF: 4-159

5. Which method is an acceptable way to prevent cross-site request forgery (XSRF)?

A. Allow vendors to implement backdoor coding techniques for easy patch distribution

B. Include more white space in the application code

C. Trap user responses by using an escaping (output encoding) technique

D. Perform input validation after the data is entered by the user but before the destination is known

Security+ SY0-401 Objective 4.1: Explain the importance of application security controls and techniques.

REF: 4-159

6. Application development security involves _____ baselines and secure coding concepts.

A. operating system

B. patch management

C. application hardening

D. application configuration

Security+ SY0-401 Objective 4.1: Explain the importance of application security controls and techniques.

REF: 4-158

7. Application _____ is intended to prevent attackers from exploiting vulnerabilities in software applications.

   A. hardening

   B. control

   C. wrapping

   D. whitelisting

   Security+ SY0-401 Objective 4.1: Explain the importance of application security controls and techniques.

   REF: 4-160

8. Which method provides the best automatic software application patch distribution solution?

   A. Utilize backdoor mechanisms for application program fix distribution

   B. Utilize an application patch management system

   C. Utilize fortification after deployment

   D. Utilize a wrapper function

   Security+ SY0-401 Objective 4.1: Explain the importance of application security controls and techniques.

   REF: 4-160

9. What expression describes the argument regarding which database technology is superior?

   A. Server-side validation vs. client-side validation

   B. NoSQL databases vs. SQL databases

   C. Cross-site scripting (XSS) vs. cross-site request forgery (XSRF)

   D. Fortification after deployment vs. tightening during initial design

   Security+ SY0-401 Objective 4.1: Explain the importance of application security controls and techniques.

   REF: 4-160

10. In client-side validation all input validations and error recovery procedures are performed by the user's _____.

    A. Internet service provider

    B. media access card (MAC)

    C. Web browser

    D. firewall security program

    Security+ SY0-401 Objective 4.1: Explain the importance of application security controls and techniques.

    REF: 4-160

4

11. Enabling full device encryption applies protection to all data stored _____.

    A. in the corporate data container

    B. in the personal data container

    C. on the device

    D. in the vendor's proprietary root folder

    Security+ SY0-401 Objective 4.2: Summarize mobile security concepts and technologies.

    REF: 10-420

12. If a lost or stolen device cannot be located, it may be necessary to perform _____, which will erase sensitive data stored on the mobile device.

    A. remote wiping

    B. remote lockout

    C. geo-fencing

    D. location beaconing

    Security+ SY0-401 Objective 4.2: Summarize mobile security concepts and technologies.

    REF: 10-422

13. Which security feature allows a mobile device to be remotely locked and sends a custom message that is displayed on the login screen?

    A. Alarm generation

    B. Location beaconing

    C. Remote wiping

    D. Remote lockout

    Security+ SY0-401 Objective 4.2: Summarize mobile security concepts and technologies.

    REF: 10-422

14. Which security feature prevents a mobile device from being used until the user enters the correct passcode such as a PIN or password?

    A. Alarm generation

    B. Location beaconing

    C. Lock screen

    D. Remote lockout

    Security+ SY0-401 Objective 4.2: Summarize mobile security concepts and technologies.

    REF: 10-418

15. Which security feature uses a mobile device's GPS to define geographical boundaries where an app can be used?

    A. Geo-fencing

    B. GEO-beaconing

    C. GEO-lockout

    D. GEO-wiping

    Security+ SY0-401 Objective 4.2: Summarize mobile security concepts and technologies.

    REF: 10-423

16. What term is sometimes used interchangeably with mobile application management (MAM)?

    A. Trusted operating system

    B. Geo-fencing

    C. Application control

    D. Mobile device management

    Security+ SY0-401 Objective 4.2: Summarize mobile security concepts and technologies.

    REF: 10-421

17. Mobile device management (MDM) can facilitate _____, or maintaining an accurate record of company owned mobile devices.

    A. inventory control

    B. baselining

    C. geo-fencing

    D. asset tracking

    Security+ SY0-401 Objective 4.2: Summarize mobile security concepts and technologies.

    REF: 10-421

18. _____ is the operation of stockrooms where mobile devices are stored prior to their dispersal to employees.

    A. Inventory control

    B. Baselining

    C. Geo-fencing

    D. Asset tracking

    Security+ SY0-401 Objective 4.2: Summarize mobile security concepts and technologies.

    REF: 10-421

4

19. _____ tools allow a device to be managed remotely by an organization.

A. Baselining

B. Mobile device management (MDM)

C. Mobile application management (MAM)

D. Application control

Security+ SY0-401 Objective 4.2: Summarize mobile security concepts and technologies.

REF: 10-421

20. Which feature should be disabled if it is not being regularly used in order to prevent bluejacking and bluesnarfing?

A. Bluetooth wireless data communication

B. Onboard camera/video

C. Geo-fencing

D. Remote locking

Security+ SY0-401 Objective 4.2: Summarize mobile security concepts and technologies.

REF: 10-418

21. _____ can be stored and managed on a mobile device using mobile device management (MDM) tools.

A. Cryptographic keys

B. Application controls

C. Wrapper functions

D. Tokens

Security+ SY0-401 Objective 4.2: Summarize mobile security concepts and technologies.

REF: 10-423

22. Which term refers to a secure repository for storing valuable authentication information on a mobile device?

A. On-boarding

B. Geo-tagging

C. Application controls

D. Credential management

Security+ SY0-401 Objective 4.2: Summarize mobile security concepts and technologies.

REF: 10-423

23. Which item describes an advantage of Bring Your Own Device (BYOD) that encourages user acceptance of the practice?

    A. Employees are responsible for their own mobile device purchases.

    B. Employees are responsible for wireless data plans.

    C. Employees are responsible for telecommunications usage for overages or extra charges.

    D. Many employees already have their own device and want the convenience of using only a single device.

    Security+ SY0-401 Objective 4.2: Summarize mobile security concepts and technologies.

    REF: 10-424

24. Which term refers to adding or allowing geographical identification data in a mobile app?

    A. Asset tracking

    B. Credential management

    C. Geo-fencing

    D. Geo-tagging

    Security+ SY0-401 Objective 4.2: Summarize mobile security concepts and technologies.

    REF: 10-423

25. On mobile devices that contain both personal and corporate data, data storage may be separated into _____ so that only sensitive data will need to be encrypted.

    A. segments

    B. baselines

    C. buckets

    D. containers

    Security+ SY0-401 Objective 4.2: Summarize mobile security concepts and technologies.

    REF: 10-420

26. Mobile device management (MDM) tools can support _____, which ensures that only preapproved apps can run on the device.

    A. change management

    B. application wrapping

    C. application whitelisting

    D. data loss prevention (DLP)

    Security+ SY0-401 Objective 4.2: Summarize mobile security concepts and technologies.

    REF: 10-423

4

27. _____ is a two-way relationship that is automatically created between parent and child domains in a Microsoft Active Directory Forest.

    A. Transitive trust

    B. Single-factor authentication

    C. Multifactor authentication

    D. Chain of custody

    Security+ SY0-401 Objective 4.2: Summarize mobile security concepts and technologies.

    REF: 12-504

28. Containerization helps companies avoid _____ privacy issues and legal concerns regarding a user's personal data stored in a Bring Your Own Device (BYOD) setting.

    A. data ownership

    B. support ownership

    C. vendor

    D. application

    Security+ SY0-401 Objective 4.2: Summarize mobile security concepts and technologies.

    REF: 10-420

29. What type of vendor-supplied software fix is universal for all customers?

    A. Hotfix

    B. Service pack

    C. Patch

    D. Repair

    Security+ SY0-401 Objective 4.2: Summarize mobile security concepts and technologies.

    REF: 4-151

30. _____ is the application of science to questions that are of interest to the legal profession.

    A. Business impact analysis (BIA)

    B. Forensics

    C. Succession planning

    D. Transitive trust

    Security+ SY0-401 Objective 4.2: Summarize mobile security concepts and technologies.

    REF: 13-545

31. Which term refers to the ability to quickly remove devices from the organization's network?

    A. Off-boarding

    B. On-boarding

    C. Remote wiping

    D. Asset isolation

    Security+ SY0-401 Objective 4.2: Summarize mobile security concepts and technologies.

    REF: 10-421

32. Which term refers to the ability to rapidly enroll new mobile devices?

    A. Inventory control

    B. Asset enrollment

    C. Off-boarding

    D. On-boarding

    Security+ SY0-401 Objective 4.2: Summarize mobile security concepts and technologies.

    REF: 10-421

33. Which characteristic applies to Bring Your Own Device (BYOD) environments?

    A. Organizations need to monitor employee telecommunications usage for overages or extra charges.

    B. BYOD increases the strain on IT help desks.

    C. By using BYOD, companies are freed from supporting a remote data network for employees.

    D. Employees are less likely to be productive while traveling or working away from the office because they are using their own device.

    Security+ SY0-401 Objective 4.2: Summarize mobile security concepts and technologies.

    REF: 10-424

34. A(n) _____ policy is a policy that defines the actions users may perform while accessing systems and networking equipment.

    A. security

    B. data storage

    C. proprietary information

    D. acceptable use

    Security+ SY0-401 Objective 4.2: Summarize mobile security concepts and technologies.

    REF: 14-581

4

35. Which operating system hardening technique significantly restricts what resources can be accessed and by whom?

    A. Implementing least privilege

    B. Reducing capabilities

    C. Kernel pruning

    D. Implementing a read-only file system

    Security+ SY0-401 Objective 4.3: Given a scenario, select the appropriate solution to establish host security.

    REF: 4-153

36. Which operating system hardening technique removes all unnecessary features that may compromise an operating system?

    A. Implementing least privilege

    B. Reducing capabilities

    C. Kernel pruning

    D. Implementing a read-only file system

    Security+ SY0-401 Objective 4.3: Given a scenario, select the appropriate solution to establish host security.

    REF: 4-153

37. Which term refers to software that can examine a computer for any infections as well as monitor computer activity and scan new documents that might contain a virus?

    A. Antispam

    B. Antivirus

    C. Antispyware

    D. Popup blocker

    Security+ SY0-401 Objective 4.3: Given a scenario, select the appropriate solution to establish host security.

    REF: 4-153

38. Which term describes spam filtering software that analyzes every word in an email and determines how frequently a word occurs in order to determine if it is spam?

    A. Fuzzing

    B. Blacklisting

    C. Whitelisting

    D. Bayesian filtering

    Security+ SY0-401 Objective 4.3: Given a scenario, select the appropriate solution to establish host security.

    REF: 4-154

39. As a separate program, popup blockers are often part of a package known as _____ that helps prevent computers from becoming infected by different types of spyware.

    A. antispam

    B. antispyware

    C. firewalls

    D. intrusion detection systems

    Security+ SY0-401 Objective 4.3: Given a scenario, select the appropriate solution to establish host security.

    REF: 4-155

40. Which term refers to a separate program or a feature incorporated within a browser that stops popup advertisements from appearing?

    A. whitelist

    B. antispyware

    C. antispam

    D. popup blocker

    Security+ SY0-401 Objective 4.3: Given a scenario, select the appropriate solution to establish host security.

    REF: 4-155

41. Which type of operating system fix requires an automatic mechanism to ensure they are installed in a timely fashion?

    A. Hotfix

    B. Service pack

    C. Patch

    D. Repair

    Security+ SY0-401 Objective 4.3: Given a scenario, select the appropriate solution to establish host security.

    REF: 4-151

42. Mobile device management (MDM) tools can support application _____, which ensures that only preapproved apps can run on the device.

    A. sandboxing

    B. blocking

    C. blacklisting

    D. whitelisting

    Security+ SY0-401 Objective 4.3: Given a scenario, select the appropriate solution to establish host security.

    REF: 4-423

4

43. A(n) _____ is an operating system (OS) that has tightened security implemented during the design and coding of the OS.

    A. locked OS

    B. restricted OS

    C. trusted OS

    D. impermeable OS

    Security+ SY0-401 Objective 4.3: Given a scenario, select the appropriate solution to establish host security.

    REF: 4-153

44. Modern operating systems include a _____ that runs as a program on a local system to protect it.

    A. virtual-based host firewall

    B. host-based application firewall

    C. virtual-based system firewall

    D. client-based host firewall

    Security+ SY0-401 Objective 4.3: Given a scenario, select the appropriate solution to establish host security.

    REF: 4-155

45. The term _____ intrusion detection system refers to a software-based application that runs on a local host computer that can detect an attack as it occurs.

    A. network

    B. host-based

    C. client-based

    D. system-based

    Security+ SY0-401 Objective 4.3: Given a scenario, select the appropriate solution to establish host security.

    REF: 7-287

46. A cable lock can be inserted into the _____ slot of a portable device and rotated so that the cable lock is secured to the device, while a cable connected to the lock can then be secured to a desk or chair.

    A. USB

    B. power

    C. security

    D. firewire

    Security+ SY0-401 Objective 4.3: Given a scenario, select the appropriate solution to establish host security.

    REF: 4-148

47. When storing a laptop, it can be placed in a _____, which is a ruggedized steel box with a lock.

    A. safe

    B. crate

    C. hutch

    D. Faraday cage

    Security+ SY0-401 Objective 4.3: Given a scenario, select the appropriate solution to establish host security.

    REF: 4-148

48. A safe is also called a _____.

    A. Faraday cage

    B. mantrap

    C. case

    D. locking cabinet

    Security+ SY0-401 Objective 4.3: Given a scenario, select the appropriate solution to establish host security.

    REF: 4-148

49. Whereas the security policy determines what must be protected, the _____ are the OS settings that impose how the policy will be enforced.

    A. host software baseline

    B. acceptable use policies

    C. data retention policies

    D. firmware settings

    Security+ SY0-401 Objective 4.3: Given a scenario, select the appropriate solution to establish host security.

    REF: 4-150

50. _____ is a means of managing and presenting computer resources by function without regard to their physical layout or location.

    A. Virtualization

    B. Sandboxing

    C. Hardening

    D. On-boarding

    Security+ SY0-401 Objective 4.3: Given a scenario, select the appropriate solution to establish host security.

    REF: 8-335

4

51. Which term refers to an instance of a particular state of a virtual machine that can be saved for later use?

A. Printout

B. Sandbox

C. Snapshot

D. Static record

Security+ SY0-401 Objective 4.3: Given a scenario, select the appropriate solution to establish host security.

REF: 8-336

52. Which term describes a patch's impact on other software or the hardware on a system?

A. Elasticity

B. Patch compatibility

C. Sandboxing

D. Security control testing

Security+ SY0-401 Objective 4.3: Given a scenario, select the appropriate solution to establish host security.

REF: 8-336

53. The term _____ refers to the ability to quickly make new virtual server machines available.

A. host availability

B. sandboxing

C. server emulation

D. patching

Security+ SY0-401 Objective 4.3: Given a scenario, select the appropriate solution to establish host security.

REF: 8-336

54. The term host _____ refers to the ability to easily expand or contract resources in a virtualized environment.

A. sandboxing

B. patching

C. elasticity

D. emulation

Security+ SY0-401 Objective 4.3: Given a scenario, select the appropriate solution to establish host security.

REF: 8-336

55. Testing the existing security configuration, known as _____, can be performed using a simulated network environment on a computer using multiple virtual machines.

    A. security load testing

    B. system investigation

    C. system challenging

    D. security control testing

    Security+ SY0-401 Objective 4.3: Given a scenario, select the appropriate solution to establish host security.

    REF: 8-337

56. Which term describes the act of loading a suspicious program into an isolated virtual machine and executing it to test for malware?

    A. Blacklisting

    B. Sandboxing

    C. Whitelisting

    D. Data wiping

    Security+ SY0-401 Objective 4.3: Given a scenario, select the appropriate solution to establish host security

    REF: 8-337

57. Which statement accurately describes a cloud storage security best practice?

    A. The cloud user is responsible for guaranteeing that the means are in place by which authorized users are given access while imposters are denied.

    B. Like most Internet-based transmissions, all transmissions to and from "the cloud" can be transmitted "in the clear."

    C. Customer's data must be properly isolated from that of other customers.

    D. The lowest level of application security must be maintained.

    Security+ SY0-401 Objective 4.4: Implement the appropriate controls to ensure data security.

    REF: 8-339

4

58. Which statement accurately describes a characteristic of a storage area network (SAN)?

    A. In an FC hard zone, all zone members are identified by a logical port number on the channel.

    B. In an FC soft zone, when a device logs in, it queries the server for all available devices and sees all devices in all available zones.

    C. A storage area network (SAN) should have its own dedicated switch that is inaccessible from clients.

    D. An FC soft zone, the hardware-based switch restricts data transfer.

    Security+ SY0-401 Objective 4.4: Implement the appropriate controls to ensure data security.

    REF: 8-321

59. The term _____ refers to a collection of data sets so large and complex that it becomes difficult to process using on-hand database management tools or traditional data processing applications.

    A. data cluster

    B. sandbox

    C. metadata

    D. big data

    Security+ SY0-401 Objective 4.4: Implement the appropriate controls to ensure data security.

    REF: 4-161

60. Which product can be used to encrypt an entire system volume?

    A. BitLocker

    B. Pretty Good Privacy

    C. New Technology File System (NTFS)

    D. Hardware Security Module (HSM)

    Security+ SY0-401 Objective 4.4: Implement the appropriate controls to ensure data security.

    REF: 5-207

61. What is the key element in securing databases?

    A. Cryptography

    B. File system

    C. Bandwidth

    D. Operating system

    Security+ SY0-401 Objective 4.4: Implement the appropriate controls to ensure data security.

    REF: 5-206

62. Which product can be used to encrypt an individual file?

    A. Hardware Security Module (HSM)

    B. Trusted Platform Module (TPM)

    C. BitLocker

    D. Pretty Good Privacy (PGP)

    Security+ SY0-401 Objective 4.4: Implement the appropriate controls to ensure data security.

    REF: 5-206

63. Which open source encryption product runs on Windows, UNIX, and Linux operating systems?

    A. Encrypting File System (EFS)

    B. BitLocker

    C. Pretty Good Privacy (PGP)

    D. GNU Privacy Guard (GPG)

    Security+ SY0-401 Objective 4.4: Implement the appropriate controls to ensure data security.

    REF: 5-206

64. Microsoft's _____ is a cryptography system for Windows operating systems that use the Windows NTFS file system.

    A. BitLocker

    B. Encrypting File System (EFS)

    C. Pretty Good Privacy (PGP)

    D. GNU Privacy Guard (GPG)

    Security+ SY0-401 Objective 4.4: Implement the appropriate controls to ensure data security.

    REF: 5-207

65. The _____ is essentially a chip on the motherboard of the computer that provides cryptographic services.

    A. firmware component

    B. capacitor module

    C. Trusted Platform Module

    D. Hardware Security Module

    Security+ SY0-401 Objective 4.4: Implement the appropriate controls to ensure data security.

    REF: 5-209

4

66. A _____ is a secure cryptographic processor.
    A. capacitor module
    B. self-encrypting hard disk drive
    C. Trusted Platform Module
    D. Hardware Security Module
    Security+ SY0-401 Objective 4.4: Implement the appropriate controls to ensure data security.
    REF: 5-209

67. Which statement applies to an encrypted hardware-based USB device?
    A. Administrators can remotely control and track activity on the devices.
    B. Encrypted hardware-based USB drives will connect to a computer immediately.
    C. All data copied to the USB flash drive must be manually encrypted.
    D. The external case may be disassembled if an attacker has the proper tools.
    Security+ SY0-401 Objective 4.4: Implement the appropriate controls to ensure data security.
    REF: 5-208

68. Self-encrypting hard disk drives (HDDs) can protect _____.
    A. selected individual files
    B. only the root folder
    C. all files stored on them
    D. only individual user folders
    Security+ SY0-401 Objective 4.4: Implement the appropriate controls to ensure data security.
    REF: 5-208

69. Actions that transmit the data across a network, like an email sent across the Internet, are called data _____.
    A. in-use
    B. in-stream
    C. in-transit
    D. at-rest
    Security+ SY0-401 Objective 4.4: Implement the appropriate controls to ensure data security.
    REF: 4-161

70. What term applies to data that is stored on electronic media?

    A. Data in-use

    B. Data in-transit

    C. Data in-stream

    D. Data at-rest

    Security+ SY0-401 Objective 4.4: Implement the appropriate controls to ensure data security.

    REF: 4-161

71. _____ involves data actions being performed by "endpoint devices," such as creating a report from a desktop computer.

    A. Data in-motion

    B. Data in-transit

    C. Data at-rest

    D. Data in-use

    Security+ SY0-401 Objective 4.4: Implement the appropriate controls to ensure data security.

    REF: 4-161

72. A(n) _____ is a set of permissions that is attached to an object.

    A. group policy

    B. access control list (ACL)

    C. mandatory access control (MAC)

    D. security identifier

    Security+ SY0-401 Objective 4.4: Implement the appropriate controls to ensure data security.

    REF: 11-454

73. Which statement represents a function of a data wiping and disposal policy?

    A. The policy describes the procedures for archiving the information.

    B. The policy describes special mechanisms for handling the information when under litigation.

    C. The policy outlines the disposal of resources that are considered confidential.

    D. The policy attempts to answer questions about how and where data is stored.

    Security+ SY0-401 Objective 4.4: Implement the appropriate controls to ensure data security.

    REF: 14-582

4

74. A data wiping and disposing policy addresses how and when data will ultimately be
    _____.
    A. erased
    B. retained
    C. stored
    D. classified
    Security+ SY0-401 Objective 4.4: Implement the appropriate controls to ensure data
    security.
    REF: 14-582

75. A data _____ policy outlines how to maintain information in the user's
    possession for a predetermined length of time.
    A. storage
    B. retention
    C. disposing
    D. wiping
    Security+ SY0-401 Objective 4.4: Implement the appropriate controls to ensure data
    security.
    REF: 14-582

76. A data _____ policy is a set of procedures designed to control and manage
    data within the organization by specifying data collection and storage.
    A. disposing
    B. storage
    C. retention
    D. wiping
    Security+ SY0-401 Objective 4.4: Implement the appropriate controls to ensure data
    security.
    REF: 14-582

77. Which static environment can be found in oil pipeline control systems?
    A. Embedded systems
    B. Mainframes
    C. Supervisory control and data acquisition
    D. On-Board Diagnostic II
    Security+ SY0-401 Objective 4.5: Compare and contrast alternative methods to
    mitigate security risks in static environments.
    REF: 4-157

78. Which static environment is a computer system with a dedicated function within a larger electrical or mechanical system?

A. Embedded

B. Cloud-based

C. Mainframe

D. Gaming console

Security+ SY0-401 Objective 4.5: Compare and contrast alternative methods to mitigate security risks in static environments.

REF: 4-156

79. Google's Android operating system is considered to be a(n) _____.

A. gaming console

B. supervisory control

C. smartphone operating system

D. embedded system

Security+ SY0-401 Objective 4.5: Compare and contrast alternative methods to mitigate security risks in static environments.

REF: 4-156

80. Which Apple smartphone operating system offers a broad range of functionality when compared to a feature phone?

A. Android

B. iOS

C. IPad

D. Mac OS X

Security+ SY0-401 Objective 4.5: Compare and contrast alternative methods to mitigate security risks in static environments.

REF: 4-156

81. Why is it difficult to mitigate security risks in mainframes?

A. The operating systems of these systems often are stripped-down versions of general-purpose operating systems.

B. The operating systems of older mainframes may lack the ability to be updated in a timely fashion by the vendor.

C. These types of systems have heightened encryption mechanisms.

D. The number of functions controlled by their microprocessors continues to decrease.

Security+ SY0-401 Objective 4.5: Compare and contrast alternative methods to mitigate security risks in static environments.

REF: 4-156

4

82. Which event provides an opening for game consoles to be exploited?

    A. The increase in network-based online gaming

    B. The implementation of On-Board Diagnostics II (OBD-II) connectors that are used for troubleshooting

    C. Their high cost reducing the frequency of replacement

    D. Expanded features such as such as a camera, an MP3 music player, and ability to send and receive short message service (SMS) text messages

    Security+ SY0-401 Objective 4.5: Compare and contrast alternative methods to mitigate security risks in static environments.

    REF: 4-156

83. Which static environment is vulnerable to an attack to the On-Board Diagnostics II (OBD-II) connector that is used for troubleshooting?

    A. In vehicle computer systems

    B. Game consoles

    C. Supervisory control and data acquisition (SCADA)

    D. Mainframes

    Security+ SY0-401 Objective 4.5: Compare and contrast alternative methods to mitigate security risks in static environments.

    REF: 4-156

84. Which defense method for avoiding attacks directed toward devices in a static environment keeps devices on their own network separated from the regular network?

    A. Security layers

    B. Application firewalls

    C. Network segmentation

    D. Wrappers

    Security+ SY0-401 Objective 4.5: Compare and contrast alternative methods to mitigate security risks in static environments.

    REF: 4-157

85. Which defense method builds security in layers around the device to avoid attacks directed toward devices in a static environment?

    A. Application firewalls

    B. Partitioning

    C. Redundancy control

    D. Security layers

    Security+ SY0-401 Objective 4.5: Compare and contrast alternative methods to mitigate security risks in static environments.

    REF: 4-157

86. By installing an application firewall on a static environment device's _____, an organization can potentially avoid attacks directed toward that device.

    A. application software

    B. media access control (MAC) card

    C. firmware

    D. operating system

    Security+ SY0-401 Objective 4.5: Compare and contrast alternative methods to mitigate security risks in static environments.

    REF: 4-157

87. When automated updates cannot be used, to avoid attacks directed toward devices in a static environment one should _____.

    A. shut the environment down until the automated system is repaired

    B. provide a means for manual software updates

    C. open a backdoor program to allow the automated updates to get applied

    D. temporarily disable the firewall system to ensure the automated updates get applied

    Security+ SY0-401 Objective 4.5: Compare and contrast alternative methods to mitigate security risks in static environments.

    REF: 4-157

88. When implementing firmware version control as a defense method to avoid attacks directed toward devices in a static environment, an organization _____.

    A. builds security in layers around the device

    B. develops a policy that keeps track of updates to firmware

    C. keeps the operating system code as basic as possible to limit overlapping or unnecessary features

    D. implements secure coding concepts and standards

    Security+ SY0-401 Objective 4.5: Compare and contrast alternative methods to mitigate security risks in static environments.

    REF: 4-157

89. Testing system functionality by using error-checking routines for preexisting system functions, also known as _____, can be used to avoid attacks directed toward devices in a static environment.

    A. wrappers

    B. firmware version control

    C. network segmentation

    D. control redundancy and diversity

    Security+ SY0-401 Objective 4.5: Compare and contrast alternative methods to mitigate security risks in static environments.

    REF: 8-158

4

90. Which defense method keeps the operating system code as basic as possible to limit overlapping or unnecessary features to avoid attacks directed toward devices in a static environment?

    A. Network segmentation

    B. Security layers

    C. Control redundancy and diversity

    D. Firmware version control

    Security+ SY0-401 Objective 4.5: Compare and contrast alternative methods to mitigate security risks in static environments.

    REF: 4-157

5.0

ACCESS CONTROL AND IDENTITY MANAGEMENT

TEST PREPARATION QUESTIONS

1. Which authentication server, developed in 1992, was originally designed for remote dial-in access to a corporate network?

   A. Kerberos

   B. Terminal Access Control Access Control System

   C. RADIUS

   D. Lightweight Directory Access Protocol

   Security+ SY0-401 Objective 5.1: Compare and contrast the function and purpose of authentication services.

   REF: 11-458

2. During a RADIUS authentication with a wireless device, a(n) _____ sends a request to an access point requesting permission to join the WLAN.

   A. authenticator

   B. supplicant

   C. proxy

   D. user

   Security+ SY0-401 Objective 5.1: Compare and contrast the function and purpose of authentication services.

   REF: 11-458

5

3. What authentication system was developed by the Massachusetts Institute of Technology (MIT) in the 1980s and is used to verify the identity of networked users?

A. Kerberos

B. RADIUS

C. Lightweight Directory Access Protocol

D. Terminal Access Control Access Control System

Security+ SY0-401 Objective 5.1: Compare and contrast the function and purpose of authentication services.

REF: 11-460

4. What type of tickets are difficult to copy, contain specific user information, restrict what a user can do, and expire after a few hours or a day?

A. Kerberos

B. RADIUS

C. LDAP

D. TACACS

Security+ SY0-401 Objective 5.1: Compare and contrast the function and purpose of authentication services.

REF: 11-460

5. What authentication service is commonly used on UNIX devices and communicates by forwarding user authentication information to a centralized server?

A. Kerberos

B. RADIUS

C. Lightweight Directory Access Protocol

D. Terminal Access Control Access Control System

Security+ SY0-401 Objective 5.1: Compare and contrast the function and purpose of authentication services.

REF: 11-460

6. A(n) _____ is a database stored on the network itself that contains information about users and network devices.

A. information base

B. directory service

C. information service

D. access directory

Security+ SY0-401 Objective 5.1: Compare and contrast the function and purpose of authentication services.

REF: 11-461

7. The directory service known as _____ has the capability to look up information by name (a white-pages service) and to browse and search for information by category (a yellow-pages service).

A. X.81

B. X.350

C. X.500

D. X.1200

Security+ SY0-401 Objective 5.1: Compare and contrast the function and purpose of authentication services.

REF: 11-461

8. A(n) _____ is an attack that constructs LDAP statements based on user input statements, allowing the attacker to retrieve information from the LDAP database or modify its content.

A. LDAP injection attack

B. RBASE attack

C. Trojan attack

D. SSL injection attack

Security+ SY0-401 Objective 5.1: Compare and contrast the function and purpose of authentication services.

REF: 11-462

9. LDAP traffic can be made secure by using Secure Sockets Layer (SSL) or Transport Layer Security (TLS). This is known as _____.

A. SSL over LDAP

B. Secure Sockets LDAP

C. Transport Layer LDAP

D. Secure LDAP

Security+ SY0-401 Objective 5.1: Compare and contrast the function and purpose of authentication services.

REF: 11-462

10. What is an Extensible Markup Language (XML) standard that allows secure web domains to exchange user authentication and authorization data?

A. GML

B. SAML

C. SMTP

D. ACL

Security+ SY0-401 Objective 5.1: Compare and contrast the function and purpose of authentication services.

REF: 11-462

5

11. Which mechanism is used in an information system for granting or denying approval to use specific resources?

A. Token

B. SID

C. Subnet mask

D. Access control

Security+ SY0-401 Objective 5.2: Given a scenario, select the appropriate authentication, authorization or access control.

REF: 11-443

12. What is the least restrictive access control model in which the owner of the object has total control over it?

A. Rule Based Access Control

B. Discretionary Access Control

C. Role Based Access Control

D. Mandatory Access Control

Security+ SY0-401 Objective 5.2: Given a scenario, select the appropriate authentication, authorization or access control.

REF: 11-446

13. One of the weaknesses of _____ is that a subject's permissions can be "inherited" by any program that the subject executes.

A. Mandatory Access Control

B. Role Based Access Control

C. Discretionary Access Control

D. Rule Based Access Control

Security+ SY0-401 Objective 5.2: Given a scenario, select the appropriate authentication, authorization or access control.

REF: 11-447

14. Which access control method assigns users' access controls strictly according to the custodian's desires?

A. Mandatory Access Control

B. Role Based Access Control

C. Discretionary Access Control

D. Rule Based Access Control

Security+ SY0-401 Objective 5.2: Given a scenario, select the appropriate authentication, authorization or access control.

REF: 11-448

15. In a system using Mandatory Access Control, every entity (laptops, files, projects, and so on) is an object and is assigned a classification _____.

    A. level

    B. clearance

    C. code

    D. label

    Security+ SY0-401 Objective 5.2: Given a scenario, select the appropriate authentication, authorization or access control.

    REF: 11-448

16. Microsoft Windows' _____ ensures data integrity by controlling access to securable objects.

    A. Mandatory Integrity Control

    B. Bell-LaPadula

    C. Biba Integrity model

    D. lattice model

    Security+ SY0-401 Objective 5.2: Given a scenario, select the appropriate authentication, authorization or access control.

    REF: 11-449

17. What is a "real-world" access control model in which access is based on a user's job function within the organization?

    A. Mandatory Integrity Control

    B. Discretionary Access Control

    C. Role Based Access Control

    D. Rule Based Access Control

    Security+ SY0-401 Objective 5.2: Given a scenario, select the appropriate authentication, authorization or access control.

    REF: 11-450

18. What is an access control model that can dynamically assign roles to subjects based on a set of rules defined by a custodian?

    A. Mandatory Integrity Control

    B. Discretionary Access Control

    C. Role Based Access Control

    D. Rule Based Access Control

    Security+ SY0-401 Objective 5.2: Given a scenario, select the appropriate authentication, authorization or access control.

    REF: 11-450

5

19. Which access control model is often used for managing user access to one or more systems, where business changes may trigger the application of the rules that specify access changes?

    A. Mandatory Integrity Control

    B. Discretionary Access Control

    C. Role Based Access Control

    D. Rule Based Access Control

    Security+ SY0-401 Objective 5.2: Given a scenario, select the appropriate authentication, authorization or access control.

    REF: 11-450

20. Which best practice of access control requires that if the fraudulent application of a process might potentially result in a breach of security, the process should be divided between two or more individuals?

    A. Implicit deny

    B. Separation of duties

    C. Job rotation

    D. Least privilege

    Security+ SY0-401 Objective 5.2: Given a scenario, select the appropriate authentication, authorization or access control.

    REF: 11-451

21. Which access control term means that only the minimum amount of privileges necessary to perform a job or function should be allocated?

    A. Least privilege

    B. Job rotation

    C. Implicit deny

    D. Separation of duties

    Security+ SY0-401 Objective 5.2: Given a scenario, select the appropriate authentication, authorization or access control.

    REF: 11-452

22. Which access control term means that if a condition is not explicitly met, the request for access is rejected?

    A. Least privilege

    B. Job rotation

    C. Implicit deny

    D. Separation of duties

    Security+ SY0-401 Objective 5.2: Given a scenario, select the appropriate authentication, authorization or access control.

    REF: 11-453

23. What is a set of permissions that is attached to an object?

    A. Secure ID

    B. Account restriction

    C. Group Policy

    D. Access control list

    Security+ SY0–401 Objective 5.2: Given a scenario, select the appropriate authentication, authorization or access control.

    REF: 11–454

24. In Windows, the access control entry (ACE) includes a(n) _____, a unique number issued to the user, group, or session that is used to identify the user in all subsequent interactions with Windows security.

    A. token

    B. SID

    C. flag

    D. access mask

    Security+ SY0–401 Objective 5.2: Given a scenario, select the appropriate authentication, authorization or access control.

    REF: 11–454

25. In Windows, the access control entry (ACE) includes a(n) _____, a value that specifies the rights that are allowed or denied, and is also used to request access rights when an object is opened.

    A. token

    B. SID

    C. flag

    D. access mask

    Security+ SY0–401 Objective 5.2: Given a scenario, select the appropriate authentication, authorization or access control.

    REF: 11–454

26. In Windows, the access control entry (ACE) includes a(n) _____ that indicates the type of ACE.

    A. SID

    B. flag

    C. access mask

    D. token

    Security+ SY0–401 Objective 5.2: Given a scenario, select the appropriate authentication, authorization or access control.

    REF: 11–454

5

27. What common type of account restriction can be used to limit when a user can log onto a system or access resources?

   A. Time-of-day restrictions

   B. Account expiration

   C. Program blocking

   D. GUI restrictions

   Security+ SY0-401 Objective 5.2: Given a scenario, select the appropriate authentication, authorization or access control.

   REF: 11-456

28. What term describes the use of more than one type of authentication credential?

   A. Multiple verification

   B. Multifactor authentication

   C. Two-factor authentication

   D. Two-time password

   Security+ SY0-401 Objective 5.2: Given a scenario, select the appropriate authentication, authorization or access control.

   REF: 12-492

29. What term describes a small device that can be affixed to a keychain with a window display that shows a code to be used for authentication?

   A. Flag

   B. Trigger

   C. Token

   D. Chip

   Security+ SY0-401 Objective 5.2: Given a scenario, select the appropriate authentication, authorization or access control.

   REF: 12-492

30. A(n) _____ is an authentication code that can be used only once or for a limited period of time.

   A. single endorsement

   B. single verification

   C. one-time password

   D. single-use ID

   Security+ SY0-401 Objective 5.2: Given a scenario, select the appropriate authentication, authorization or access control.

   REF: 12-492

31. What term describes a one-time password that changes after a set period of time?

    A. Time-based one-time password (TOTP)

    B. Token-based one-time password (TOTP)

    C. Flag-based one-time password (FOTP)

    D. HMAC-based one-time password (HOTP)

    Security+ SY0-401 Objective 5.2: Given a scenario, select the appropriate authentication, authorization or access control.

    REF: 12-492

32. What is an "event-driven," one-time password that changes when a specific event occurs, such as when a user enters a personal identification number (PIN) on the token's keypad, triggering the token to create a random code?

    A. Time-based one-time password (TOTP)

    B. Token-based one-time password (TOTP)

    C. Flag-based one-time password (FOTP)

    D. HMAC-based one-time password (HOTP)

    Security+ SY0-401 Objective 5.2: Given a scenario, select the appropriate authentication, authorization or access control.

    REF: 12-493

33. What is a U.S. Department of Defense (DoD) smart card that is used for identification of active-duty and reserve military personnel along with civilian employees and special contractors?

    A. Personal Identity Verification card

    B. common access card (CAC)

    C. Secure ID card

    D. Government Smart Card

    Security+ SY0-401 Objective 5.2: Given a scenario, select the appropriate authentication, authorization or access control.

    REF: 12-494

34. The smart card standard covering all U.S. government employees is the
    _____.

    A. Secure ID

    B. Lightweight Directory Access Protocol

    C. Personal Identity Verification

    D. Secure LDAP

    Security+ SY0-401 Objective 5.2: Given a scenario, select the appropriate authentication, authorization or access control.

    REF: 12-494

5

35. What type of card contains an integrated circuit chip that can hold information, which can then be used as part of the authentication process?

    A. smart card

    B. mag stripe card

    C. access card

    D. IC card

    Security+ SY0-401 Objective 5.2: Given a scenario, select the appropriate authentication, authorization or access control.

    REF: 12-494

36. What term describes the use of one authentication credential to access multiple accounts or applications?

    A. Single login

    B. Central ID

    C. Central login

    D. Single sign-on

    Security+ SY0-401 Objective 5.2: Given a scenario, select the appropriate authentication, authorization or access control.

    REF: 12-500

37. What is a decentralized open-source FIM without requirements for specific software to be installed on the desktop?

    A. OpenID

    B. OAuth

    C. LiveID

    D. .NET Passport

    Security+ SY0-401 Objective 5.2: Given a scenario, select the appropriate authentication, authorization or access control.

    REF: 12-501

38. The open source service_____ permits users to share resources stored on one site with a second site without forwarding their authentication credentials to the other site.

    A. OpenID

    B. OAuth

    C. LiveID

    D. .NET Passport

    Security+ SY0-401 Objective 5.2: Given a scenario, select the appropriate authentication, authorization or access control.

    REF: 12-502

39. Token credentials include a _____, which is a unique, random string of characters that is encrypted to protect the token from being used by unauthorized parties.

    A. smart card

    B. rainbow table

    C. salt ID

    D. token identifier

    Security+ SY0–401 Objective 5.2: Given a scenario, select the appropriate authentication, authorization or access control.

    REF: 12-502

40. What two-way relationship is automatically created between parent and child domains in a Microsoft Active Directory Forest?

    A. Lockout

    B. Federated identity management

    C. Transitive trust

    D. Shared sign-on

    Security+ SY0–401 Objective 5.2: Given a scenario, select the appropriate authentication, authorization or access control.

    REF: 12-504

41. What term describes the five elements that can prove the genuineness of a user: what you know, what you have, what you are, what you do, and where you are?

    A. Bcrypt identifiers

    B. Behavioral biometrics

    C. Authentication factors

    D. Key credentials

    Security+ SY0–401 Objective 5.2: Given a scenario, select the appropriate authentication, authorization or access control.

    REF: 12-481

42. What is a secret combination of letters, numbers, and/or characters of which only the user should have knowledge?

    A. Rainbow table

    B. Password

    C. Username

    D. Token

    Security+ SY0–401 Objective 5.2: Given a scenario, select the appropriate authentication, authorization or access control.

    REF: 12-481

5

43. Phishing, shoulder surfing, and dumpster diving represent _____ attacks.

    A. brute force

    B. dictionary

    C. social engineering

    D. man-in-the-middle

    Security+ SY0-401 Objective 5.2: Given a scenario, select the appropriate authentication, authorization or access control.

    REF: 12-484

44. With _____, attackers steal the file of password digests and then load that file onto their own computers so that they can attempt to discover the passwords by comparing the stolen digest passwords with candidate digests that they have created.

    A. offline cracking

    B. social engineering

    C. brute force attacks

    D. hybrid attacks

    Security+ SY0-401 Objective 5.2: Given a scenario, select the appropriate authentication, authorization or access control.

    REF: 12-484

45. In an automated _____ attack, every possible combination of letters, numbers, and characters is used to create candidate digests that are then matched against those in the stolen digest file.

    A. dictionary

    B. hybrid

    C. social engineering

    D. brute force

    Security+ SY0-401 Objective 5.2: Given a scenario, select the appropriate authentication, authorization or access control.

    REF: 12-484

46. A dictionary attack that uses a set of dictionary words and compares it with the stolen digests is known as a _____, because one known digest (dictionary word) is compared to an unknown digest (stolen digest).

    A. birthday attack

    B. pre-image attack

    C. hybrid attack

    D. brute force

    Security+ SY0-401 Objective 5.2: Given a scenario, select the appropriate authentication, authorization or access control.

    REF: 12-485

47. What type of attack combines a dictionary attack with a brute force attack and will slightly alter dictionary words by adding numbers to the end of the password, spelling words backward, slightly misspelling words, or including special characters such as @, $, !, or %?

    A. hybrid

    B. malware

    C. social engineering

    D. phishing

    Security+ SY0-401 Objective 5.2: Given a scenario, select the appropriate authentication, authorization or access control.

    REF: 12-486

48. _____ make password attacks easier by creating a large pregenerated data set of candidate digests.

    A. Dictionary tables

    B. Keystroke tables

    C. Username tables

    D. Rainbow tables

    Security+ SY0-401 Objective 5.2: Given a scenario, select the appropriate authentication, authorization or access control.

    REF: 12-486

49. The _____ uses a cryptographic one-way function (OWF): instead of encrypting the password with another key, the password itself is the key.

    A. LAN Manager hash

    B. MD-5 hash

    C. Technology LAN Manager hash

    D. SHA-1 hash

    Security+ SY0-401 Objective 5.2: Given a scenario, select the appropriate authentication, authorization or access control.

    REF: 12-490

50. What term describes a password hashing algorithm that requires significantly more time than standard hashing algorithms to create the digest?

    A. Multifactor authentication

    B. Key stretching

    C. Bycrypt authentication

    D. Token stretching

    Security+ SY0-401 Objective 5.2: Given a scenario, select the appropriate authentication, authorization or access control.

    REF: 12-491

5

51. What term describes a random string that is used in hash algorithms?

    A. Bcrypt

    B. Token

    C. Rainbow table

    D. Salt

    Security+ SY0-401 Objective 5.2: Given a scenario, select the appropriate authentication, authorization or access control.

    REF: 12-491

52. _____ make dictionary attacks and brute force attacks for cracking large number of passwords much slower and limits the impact of rainbow tables.

    A. Bcrypts

    B. Tokens

    C. Salts

    D. Smart cards

    Security+ SY0-401 Objective 5.2: Given a scenario, select the appropriate authentication, authorization or access control.

    REF: 12-491

53. Two popular key stretching password hash algorithms are _____.

    A. bcrypt and MD5

    B. SHA-256 and SHA-512

    C. PBKDF2 and bcrypt

    D. SHA-512 and PBKDF2

    Security+ SY0-401 Objective 5.2: Given a scenario, select the appropriate authentication, authorization or access control.

    REF: 12-494

54. What type of scanner has become the most common type of standard biometric device?

    A. Voice recognition

    B. Iris

    C. Retina

    D. Fingerprint

    Security+ SY0-401 Objective 5.2: Given a scenario, select the appropriate authentication, authorization or access control.

    REF: 12-495

55. What type of behavioral biometrics considers dwell time and flight time?

    A. Keystroke dynamics

    B. Voice recognition

    C. Geolocation

    D. Single sign-on

    Security+ SY0–401 Objective 5.2: Given a scenario, select the appropriate authentication, authorization or access control.

    REF: 12-498

56. What term describes the use of technology to identify the location of a person or object using technology?

    A. Pinpoint tracking

    B. Time-Location Resource Monitoring

    C. Geolocation

    D. Site biometrics

    Security+ SY0–401 Objective 5.2: Given a scenario, select the appropriate authentication, authorization or access control.

    REF: 12-499

57. _____ is a single sign-on for networks owned by different organizations.

    A. Geolocation

    B. Federated identity management

    C. New Technology LAN Manager

    D. PBKDF2

    Security+ SY0–401 Objective 5.2: Given a scenario, select the appropriate authentication, authorization or access control.

    REF: 12-500

58. _____ holds the promise of reducing the number of usernames and passwords that users must memorize (potentially, to just one).

    A. PBKDF2

    B. Salt

    C. Key stretching

    D. Single sign-on

    Security+ SY0–401 Objective 5.2: Given a scenario, select the appropriate authentication, authorization or access control.

    REF: 12-500

5

59. What identity system is a URL-based identity system that creates a webpage that is used for authentication?

A. Microsoft Account

B. OpenID

C. Windows Live ID

D. Open Authorization

Security+ SY0-401 Objective 5.2: Given a scenario, select the appropriate authentication, authorization or access control.

REF: 12-501

60. Which single sign-on system relies on token credentials?

A. Microsoft Account

B. OpenID

C. Open Authorization

D. Windows Live ID

Security+ SY0-401 Objective 5.2: Given a scenario, select the appropriate authentication, authorization or access control.

REF: 12-502

61. _____ is a weak authentication protocol that has been replaced by the Extensible Authentication Protocol (EAP).

A. Challenge-Handshake Authentication Protocol

B. Lightweight EAP

C. Temporal Key Integrity Protocol

D. Network Authentication Protocol

Security+ SY0-401 Objective 5.2: Given a scenario, select the appropriate authentication, authorization or access control.

REF: 9-383

62. _____ is a proprietary EAP method developed by Cisco Systems, and is based on the Microsoft implementation of CHAP.

A. Protected EAP

B. Enhanced EAP

C. Lightweight EAP

D. Verified EAP

Security+ SY0-401 Objective 5.2: Given a scenario, select the appropriate authentication, authorization or access control.

REF: 9-383

63. _____ creates an encrypted channel between the client and the authentication server. The channel then protects the subsequent user authentication exchange.

    A. Protected EAP

    B. EAP-FAST

    C. Lightweight EAP

    D. EAP-SIM

    Security+ SY0-401 Objective 5.2: Given a scenario, select the appropriate authentication, authorization or access control.

    REF: 9-383

64. Which EAP protocol securely tunnels any credential form for authentication (such as a password or a token) using TLS?

    A. Protected EAP

    B. EAP-FAST

    C. Lightweight EAP

    D. EAP-SIM

    Security+ SY0-401 Objective 5.2: Given a scenario, select the appropriate authentication, authorization or access control.

    REF: 9-384

65. Which EAP protocol is based on the subscriber identity module card installed in mobile phones and other devices that use Global System for Mobile Communications (GSM) networks?

    A. Protected EAP

    B. EAP-FAST

    C. Lightweight EAP

    D. EAP-SIM

    Security+ SY0-401 Objective 5.2: Given a scenario, select the appropriate authentication, authorization or access control.

    REF: 9-384

66. What term describes a Microsoft Windows feature that provides centralized management and configuration of computers and remote users using the Microsoft directory services Active Directory (AD)?

    A. Group Policy

    B. Account restriction

    C. Access control list

    D. Account expiration

    Security+ SY0-401 Objective 5.3: Install and configure security controls when performing account management, based on best practices.

    REF: 11-455

5

67. _____ is usually used in enterprise environments to enforce access control by restricting user actions that may pose a security risk, such as changing access to certain folders or downloading executable files.

A. Group Policy

B. Kerberos

C. Job rotation

D. Secure LDAP

Security+ SY0-401 Objective 5.3: Install and configure security controls when performing account management, based on best practices.

REF: 11-455

68. A(n) _____ is used to configure settings for systems that are not part of Active Directory.

A. access mask

B. Local Group Policy

C. Secure LDAP

D. SID

Security+ SY0-401 Objective 5.3: Install and configure security controls when performing account management, based on best practices.

REF: 11-455

69. _____ can control an object's script for logging on and off the system, folder redirection, Internet Explorer settings, and Windows Registry settings.

A. Group Policy

B. RADIUS

C. Secure LDAP

D. Kerberos

Security+ SY0-401 Objective 5.3: Install and configure security controls when performing account management, based on best practices.

REF: 11-455

70. As a means of controlling orphaned and dormant accounts, _____ can be set for a specific date or based on a specific number of days of inactivity.

A. login monitors

B. password expiration

C. account expiration

D. user authentication

Security+ SY0-401 Objective 5.3: Install and configure security controls when performing account management, based on best practices.

REF: 11-456

71. In a Windows environment, time-of-day restrictions can be set through a(n) _____.

    A. orphaned account

    B. dormant account

    C. login control

    D. Group Policy

    Security+ SY0-401 Objective 5.3: Install and configure security controls when performing account management, based on best practices.

    REF: 11-456

72. _____ are user accounts that remain active after an employee has left an organization.

    A. Reserved accounts

    B. Orphaned accounts

    C. Guest accounts

    D. Dormant accounts

    Security+ SY0-401 Objective 5.3: Install and configure security controls when performing account management, based on best practices.

    REF: 11-456

73. A(n) _____ is one that has not been accessed for a lengthy period of time.

    A. guest account

    B. orphaned account

    C. dormant account

    D. widowed account

    Security+ SY0-401 Objective 5.3: Install and configure security controls when performing account management, based on best practices.

    REF: 11-456

74. What term indicates when an account is no longer active?

    A. User expiration

    B. Password expiration

    C. Access expiration

    D. Account expiration

    Security+ SY0-401 Objective 5.3: Install and configure security controls when performing account management, based on best practices.

    REF: 11-457

5

75. _____ sets the time when a user must create a new password in order to access his account.

A. User expiration

B. Password expiration

C. Access expiration

D. Account expiration

Security+ SY0-401 Objective 5.3: Install and configure security controls when performing account management, based on best practices.

REF: 11-457

76. What type of accounts, if left unchecked, can provide an avenue for an attacker to exploit without the fear of the actual user or a system administrator noticing?

A. Orphaned accounts

B. Admin accounts

C. Dormant accounts

D. Guest accounts

Security+ SY0-401 Objective 5.3: Install and configure security controls when performing account management, based on best practices.

REF: 11-457

77. A strong password should be a minimum of _____ characters in length.

A. 6

B. 9

C. 11

D. 15

Security+ SY0-401 Objective 5.3: Install and configure security controls when performing account management, based on best practices.

REF: 11-488

78. One way to make passwords stronger is to use _____.

A. two-digit combinations

B. dictionary words with dates

C. nonkeyboard characters

D. repeat characters

Security+ SY0-401 Objective 5.3: Install and configure security controls when performing account management, based on best practices.

REF: 11-488

79. Good credential management includes _____.

    A. recycling old passwords that qualified as very strong

    B. password protecting the ROM BIOS

    C. physically locking the keyboard

    D. keeping a written list of passwords in an off-site location

    Security+ SY0-401 Objective 5.3: Install and configure security controls when performing account management, based on best practices.

    REF: 11-489

80. Password _____ allow users to create and store multiple strong passwords in a single user "vault" file that is protected by one strong master password.

    A. management applications

    B. generating applications

    C. hashing algorithms

    D. policy applications

    Security+ SY0-401 Objective 5.3: Install and configure security controls when performing account management, based on best practices.

    REF: 11-490

81. In a Microsoft Windows Group Policy environment, which password policy setting determines the number of unique new passwords a user must use before an old password can be reused?

    A. Minimum password age

    B. Enforce password history

    C. Maximum password age

    D. Minimum password length

    Security+ SY0-401 Objective 5.3: Install and configure security controls when performing account management, based on best practices.

    REF: 12-503

82. In a Microsoft Windows Group Policy environment, which password policy setting determines how many days a password can be used before the user is required to change it?

    A. Minimum password age

    B. Enforce password history

    C. Maximum password age

    D. Minimum password length

    Security+ SY0-401 Objective 5.3: Install and configure security controls when performing account management, based on best practices.

    REF: 12-503

83. In a Microsoft Windows Group Policy environment, which password policy setting determines the minimum number of characters a password can have?

    A. Maximum password length

    B. Enforce password history

    C. Maximum password age

    D. Minimum password length

    Security+ SY0-401 Objective 5.3: Install and configure security controls when performing account management, based on best practices.

    REF: 12-503

84. In a Microsoft Windows Group Policy environment, which password policy setting determines how many days a new password must be kept before the user can change it (from 0 to 999)?

    A. Minimum password age

    B. Store passwords using reversible encryption

    C. Maximum password age

    D. Minimum password length

    Security+ SY0-401 Objective 5.3: Install and configure security controls when performing account management, based on best practices.

    REF: 12-503

85. In a Microsoft Windows Group Policy environment, which password policy setting provides support for applications that use protocols which require knowledge of the user's password for authentication purposes?

    A. Minimum password age

    B. Store passwords using reversible encryption

    C. Passwords must meet complexity requirements

    D. Minimum password length

    Security+ SY0-401 Objective 5.3: Install and configure security controls when performing account management, based on best practices.

    REF: 12-503

86. In a Microsoft Windows Group Policy environment, which password policy setting would prevent creating a password which included the user's account name or parts of the user's full name?

    A. Minimum password age

    B. Store passwords using reversible encryption

    C. Maximum password age

    D. Passwords must meet complexity requirements

    Security+ SY0-401 Objective 5.3: Install and configure security controls when performing account management, based on best practices.

    REF: 12-503

87. Which account lockout policy setting determines the length of time before the account lockout threshold setting resets to zero?

    A. Account lockout threshold

    B. Minimum lockout period

    C. Account lockout duration

    D. Reset account lockout counter after

    Security+ SY0-401 Objective 5.3: Install and configure security controls when performing account management, based on best practices.

    REF: 12-504

88. Which account lockout policy setting determines the number of failed login attempts before a lockout occurs?

    A. Account lockout threshold

    B. Minimum lockout period

    C. Account lockout duration

    D. Reset account lockout counter after

    Security+ SY0-401 Objective 5.3: Install and configure security controls when performing account management, based on best practices.

    REF: 12-504

89. Which account lockout policy setting determines the length of time a locked account remains unavailable before a user can try to log in again?

    A. Account lockout threshold

    B. Minimum lockout period

    C. Account lockout duration

    D. Reset account lockout counter after

    Security+ SY0-401 Objective 5.3: Install and configure security controls when performing account management, based on best practices.

    REF: 12-504

90. Which account lockout policy setting has a recommended setting of 30 invalid attempts?

    A. Account lockout threshold

    B. Minimum lockout period

    C. Account lockout duration

    D. Reset account lockout counter after

    Security+ SY0-401 Objective 5.3: Install and configure security controls when performing account management, based on best practices.

    REF: 12-504

5

6.0

CRYPTOGRAPHY

TEST PREPARATION QUESTIONS

1. Which term describes the science of transforming information into a secure form so that unauthorized persons cannot access it?

   A. Lithography

   B. Cryptography

   C. Lexicography

   D. Steganography

   Security+ SY0-401 Objective 6.1: Given a scenario, utilize general cryptography concepts.

   REF: 5-186

2. Which term describes the art of hiding the existence of data?

   A. Steganography

   B. Lithography

   C. Cryptography

   D. Lexicography

   Security+ SY0-401 Objective 6.1: Given a scenario, utilize general cryptography concepts.

   REF: 5-186

6

3. Changing the original text into a secret message using cryptography is known as
_____.

A. transcription

B. decryption

C. translation

D. encryption

Security+ SY0-401 Objective 6.1: Given a scenario, utilize general cryptography concepts.

REF: 5-186

4. Which term defines data that is to be encrypted and is the result of decryption as well?

A. Puretext

B. Plaintext

C. Ciphertext

D. Cryptotext

Security+ SY0-401 Objective 6.1: Given a scenario, utilize general cryptography concepts.

REF: 5-186

5. What is the process of proving that a user has performed an action, such as sending an email message?

A. Integrity check

B. Validity challenge

C. Authentication

D. Non-repudiation

Security+ SY0-401 Objective 6.1: Given a scenario, utilize general cryptography concepts.

REF: 5-188

6. Whereas a stream cipher works on one character at a time, a _____ manipulates an entire group of plaintext at one time.

A. transposition cipher

B. permutation cipher

C. block cipher

D. packet cipher

Security+ SY0-401 Objective 6.1: Given a scenario, utilize general cryptography concepts.

REF: 5-190

7. Which type of cipher is fast when the amount of text is short, but can consume much more processing power if the text is lengthy?

A. Stream cipher

B. Block cipher

C. Hash cipher

D. Pseudorandom cipher

Security+ SY0-401 Objective 6.1: Given a scenario, utilize general cryptography concepts.

REF: 5-190

8. Which cryptographic algorithm creates a unique "digital fingerprint" of a set of data?

A. Hash

B. Stream cipher

C. Checksum

D. Block cipher

Security+ SY0-401 Objective 6.1: Given a scenario, utilize general cryptography concepts.

REF: 5-190

9. Which cryptographic algorithm creates a value in which it is impossible to determine the original set of data from that value?

A. Pseudorandom cipher

B. Block cipher

C. Stream cipher

D. Hashing

Security+ SY0-401 Objective 6.1: Given a scenario, utilize general cryptography concepts.

REF: 5-191

10. Which type of cryptographic algorithm uses the same single key to encrypt and decrypt a document?

A. Block cipher

B. Symmetric

C. Asymmetric

D. Public key

Security+ SY0-401 Objective 6.1: Given a scenario, utilize general cryptography concepts.

REF: 5-194

6

11. Symmetric encryption is also called _____.
    A. private key cryptography
    B. stream cryptography
    C. public key cryptography
    D. block cryptography
    Security+ SY0-401 Objective 6.1: Given a scenario, utilize general cryptography concepts.
    REF: 5-195

12. Which encryption technique uses two keys instead of only one to avoid distributing and maintaining a secure single key?
    A. Stream cryptography
    B. Symmetric cryptography
    C. Asymmetric cryptography
    D. Double key cryptography
    Security+ SY0-401 Objective 6.1: Given a scenario, utilize general cryptography concepts.
    REF: 5-199

13. Electronic verification of the sender in a communication can be provided by (a) _____.
    A. digital signature
    B. symmetric encryption
    C. private key cryptography
    D. single key cryptography
    Security+ SY0-401 Objective 6.1: Given a scenario, utilize general cryptography concepts.
    REF: 5-200

14. Which type of cryptography uses smaller key sizes and is therefore better suited for mobile devices?
    A. RSA cryptography
    B. Elliptic curve cryptography
    C. Blowfish cryptography
    D. Rivest cipher
    Security+ SY0-401 Objective 6.1: Given a scenario, utilize general cryptography concepts.
    REF: 5-204

15. Which type of cryptography attempts to use the unusual and unique behavior of microscopic objects to enable users to securely develop and share keys as well as to detect eavesdropping?

    A. String theory cryptography

    B. Lattice-based cryptography

    C. Elliptic curve cryptography

    D. Quantum cryptography

    Security+ SY0-401 Objective 6.1: Given a scenario, utilize general cryptography concepts.

    REF: 5-205

16. Which term describes exchanging cryptographic keys outside of the normal communication channels?

    A. Dedicated-line key exchange

    B. Discrete-channel key exchange

    C. Out-of-band key exchange

    D. Private-band key exchange

    Security+ SY0-401 Objective 6.1: Given a scenario, utilize general cryptography concepts.

    REF: 5-205

17. Which key exchange solution within the normal communications channel of cryptography requires Alice and Bob to each agree upon a large prime number and related integer allowing them to separately create the same key?

    A. Ephemeral keys

    B. Perfect forward secrecy

    C. Diffie-Hellman

    D. SHA

    Security+ SY0-401 Objective 6.1: Given a scenario, utilize general cryptography concepts.

    REF: 5-206

18. Which term defines temporary keys that are used only once and then discarded?

    A. Ephemeral keys

    B. Random keys

    C. Asymmetric keys

    D. Static keys

    Security+ SY0-401 Objective 6.1: Given a scenario, utilize general cryptography concepts.

    REF: 5-206

6

19. Public key systems that generate random public keys that are different for each session are called _____.

    A. Private key

    B. In-band key exchange

    C. Out-of-band key exchange

    D. Perfect forward secrecy

    Security+ SY0-401 Objective 6.1: Given a scenario, utilize general cryptography concepts.

    REF: 5-206

20. Which term refers to a process in which keys are managed by a third party, such as a trusted CA?

    A. Perfect forward secrecy

    B. Key escrow

    C. Digital certificate

    D. Digital signature

    Security+ SY0-401 Objective 6.1: Given a scenario, utilize general cryptography concepts.

    REF: 6-247

21. What characteristic distinguishes HMAC from MAC?

    A. HMAC authenticates the sender of the message.

    B. HMAC ensures confidentiality of the message.

    C. HMAC ensures that data is accessible to authorized users.

    D. HMAC applies a hash function to both the key and the message.

    Security+ SY0-401 Objective 6.2: Given a scenario, use appropriate cryptographic methods.

    REF: 5-191

22. What is the current version of the Message Digest algorithm?

    A. MD2

    B. MD4

    C. MD5

    D. MD6

    Security+ SY0-401 Objective 6.2: Given a scenario, use appropriate cryptographic methods.

    REF: 5-193

23. Which family of hashing algorithms comprises SHA-224, SHA-256, SHA-384, and SHA-512?

    A. SHA-0

    B. SHA-1

    C. SHA-2

    D. SHA-3

    Security+ SY0-401 Objective 6.2: Given a scenario, use appropriate cryptographic methods.

    REF: 5-193

24. What was the winning algorithm of 2007 NIST's SHA-3 contest?

    A. Whirlpool

    B. Keccak

    C. Rijndael

    D. RIPEMD

    Security+ SY0-401 Objective 6.2: Given a scenario, use appropriate cryptographic methods.

    REF: 5-193

25. What is the size of the digest created by Whirlpool?

    A. 256 bits

    B. 512 bits

    C. 1024 bits

    D. 2048 bits

    Security+ SY0-401 Objective 6.2: Given a scenario, use appropriate cryptographic methods.

    REF: 3-112

26. Which hashing algorithm features two different and independent parallel chains of computation, the results of which are then combined at the end of the process?

    A. RIPEMD

    B. Keccak

    C. Rijndael

    D. Whirlpool

    Security+ SY0-401 Objective 6.2: Given a scenario, use appropriate cryptographic methods.

    REF: 5-194

6

27. What is the key size for DES?

A. 56 bits

B. 128 bits

C. 220 bits

D. 256 bits

Security+ SY0-401 Objective 6.2: Given a scenario, use appropriate cryptographic methods.

REF: 5-196

28. DES is a _____ cipher that divides plaintext into 64-bit blocks and then executes the algorithm 16 times.

A. byte

B. packet

C. stream

D. block

Security+ SY0-401 Objective 6.2: Given a scenario, use appropriate cryptographic methods.

REF: 5-196

29. Which encryption algorithm was designed to replace DES and uses three rounds of encryption instead of one?

A. 3DES

B. AES

C. Blowfish

D. Twofish

Security+ SY0-401 Objective 6.2: Given a scenario, use appropriate cryptographic methods.

REF: 5-196

30. What is currently the official standard for symmetric encryption by the U.S. government?

A. DES

B. AES

C. 3DES

D. Blowfish

Security+ SY0-401 Objective 6.2: Given a scenario, use appropriate cryptographic methods.

REF: 5-197

31. What is the maximum key size for RC4?

    A. 56 bits

    B. 64 bits

    C. 128 bits

    D. 256 bits

    Security+ SY0-401 Objective 6.2: Given a scenario, use appropriate cryptographic methods.

    REF: 5-198

32. Which block cipher processes 64 bits with a 128-bit key with eight rounds?

    A. Blowfish

    B. RC4

    C. 3DES

    D. IDEA

    Security+ SY0-401 Objective 6.2: Given a scenario, use appropriate cryptographic methods.

    REF: 5-198

33. Which block cipher algorithm, designed to run efficiently on 32-bit computers, operates on 64-bit blocks and can have a key length from 32 to 448 bits?

    A. DES

    B. RC6

    C. IDEA

    D. Blowfish

    Security+ SY0-401 Objective 6.2: Given a scenario, use appropriate cryptographic methods.

    REF: 5-198

34. Which algorithm is a derivation of Blowfish?

    A. OTP

    B. IDEA

    C. Twofish

    D. TruFish

    Security+ SY0-401 Objective 6.2: Given a scenario, use appropriate cryptographic methods.

    REF: 5-198

6

35. What is the only known method to perform encryption that cannot be broken mathematically?

    A. Block cipher

    B. One-time pad

    C. Stream cipher

    D. Electronic Code Book

    Security+ SY0-401 Objective 6.2: Given a scenario, use appropriate cryptographic methods.

    REF: 5-198

36. What is the most common asymmetric cryptography algorithm?

    A. RSA

    B. ElGamal

    C. SHA

    D. SSH

    Security+ SY0-401 Objective 6.2: Given a scenario, use appropriate cryptographic methods.

    REF: 5-202

37. NTRUEncrypt uses _____ cryptography based on a set of points in space.

    A. sloping curves

    B. elliptic curves

    C. lattice-based

    D. large prime numbers

    Security+ SY0-401 Objective 6.2: Given a scenario, use appropriate cryptographic methods.

    REF: 5-204

38. Which algorithm uses elliptic curve cryptography instead of prime numbers in its computation?

    A. OTP

    B. DHE

    C. DH

    D. ECDH

    Security+ SY0-401 Objective 6.2: Given a scenario, use appropriate cryptographic methods.

    REF: 5-206

39. What is a distinguishing feature of the DHE method of key exchange?

    A. DHE uses ephemeral keys.

    B. DHE modifies the same public key in multiple sessions using intermediate values.

    C. DHE applies methods of quantum cryptography.

    D. DHE applies a variation of the RSA algorithm.

    Security+ SY0-401 Objective 6.2: Given a scenario, use appropriate cryptographic methods.

    REF: 5-206

40. Which program is one the most widely used commercial asymmetric cryptography systems for files and email messages on Windows systems?

    A. GPG

    B. PGP

    C. IDEA

    D. WGP

    Security+ SY0-401 Objective 6.2: Given a scenario, use appropriate cryptographic methods.

    REF: 5-206

41. What is the open source version of PGP?

    A. WGP

    B. GPG

    C. IDEA

    D. EFS

    Security+ SY0-401 Objective 6.2: Given a scenario, use appropriate cryptographic methods.

    REF: 5-206

42. What algorithm is used by PGP for protecting digital signatures?

    A. RSA

    B. IDEA

    C. 3DES

    D. ElGamal

    Security+ SY0-401 Objective 6.2: Given a scenario, use appropriate cryptographic methods.

    REF: 5-207

6

43. Which algorithm was designed in 1994 to create an encrypted data path between a client and a server that could be used on any platform or operating system?

    A. Transport Layer Security (TLS)

    B. Secure Sockets Layer (SSL)

    C. Secure Shell (SSH)

    D. Hypertext Transport Protocol Secure (HTTPS)

    Security+ SY0-401 Objective 6.2: Given a scenario, use appropriate cryptographic methods.

    REF: 6-249

44. What is the current version of SSL?

    A. 1.2

    B. 2.1

    C. 2.2

    D. 3.0

    Security+ SY0-401 Objective 6.2: Given a scenario, use appropriate cryptographic methods

    REF: 6-249

45. Which algorithm served as the basis for TLS v1.0?

    A. SSH v2.0

    B. SSL v3.1

    C. SHA-2

    D. SSL v3.0

    Security+ SY0-401 Objective 6.2: Given a scenario, use appropriate cryptographic methods.

    REF: 6-249

46. Which term describes a named combination of the encryption, authentication, and message authentication code (MAC) algorithms that are used with SSL and TLS?

    A. Cipher suite

    B. Cipher family

    C. Crypto suite

    D. Crypto family

    Security+ SY0-401 Objective 6.2: Given a scenario, use appropriate cryptographic methods.

    REF: 6-250

47. In general, at least how many bits are required for a key to be considered good?

    A. 512

    B. 1024

    C. 2048

    D. 4096

    Security+ SY0-401 Objective 6.2: Given a scenario, use appropriate cryptographic methods.

    REF: 6-250

48. What is an encrypted alternative to the Telnet protocol that is used to access remote computers?

    A. SSL

    B. TLS

    C. SSH

    D. IPsec

    Security+ SY0-401 Objective 6.2: Given a scenario, use appropriate cryptographic methods.

    REF: 6-250

49. What three utilities comprise SSH?

    A. login, telnet, and cp

    B. rlogin, rsh, and rcp

    C. slogin, ssh, and scp

    D. login, sh, and cp

    Security+ SY0-401 Objective 6.2: Given a scenario, use appropriate cryptographic methods

    REF: 6-250

50. Securing the Hypertext Transport Protocol with TLS and SSL is commonly known as _____.

    A. IPsec

    B. HTTPS

    C. SSH

    D. SHTTP

    Security+ SY0-401 Objective 6.2: Given a scenario, use appropriate cryptographic methods.

    REF: 6-251

6

51. Which algorithm encrypts and authenticates each IP packet of a session between hosts or networks?

    A. IPsec

    B. TLS

    C. SSL

    D. HTTPS

    Security+ SY0-401 Objective 6.2: Given a scenario, use appropriate cryptographic methods.

    REF: 6-251

52. Which encryption mode supported by IPsec encrypts only the data portion (payload) of each packet yet leaves the header unencrypted?

    A. transparent

    B. confidential

    C. tunnel

    D. transport

    Security+ SY0-401 Objective 6.2: Given a scenario, use appropriate cryptographic methods.

    REF: 6-252

53. Which protocol is used by IPsec to achieve confidentiality?

    A. Encapsulating Security Payload (ESP)

    B. Authentication Header (AH)

    C. Internet Security Association and Key Management Protocol (ISAKMP)

    D. Secure Sockets Layer (SSL)

    Security+ SY0-401 Objective 6.2: Given a scenario, use appropriate cryptographic methods.

    REF: 6-252

54. In October 2003 the Wi-Fi Alliance introduced _____ to offer secure wireless access.

    A. IPsec

    B. WPA2

    C. WPA

    D. WEP

    Security+ SY0-401 Objective 6.2: Given a scenario, use appropriate cryptographic methods.

    REF: 9-380

55. What is the core technology behind WPA?

    A. IPsec

    B. TKIP

    C. PSK

    D. TLS

    Security+ SY0-401 Objective 6.2: Given a scenario, use appropriate cryptographic methods.

    REF: 9-380

56. What technology does WPA use to authenticate users?

    A. IPsec

    B. TKIP

    C. MIC

    D. PSK

    Security+ SY0-401 Objective 6.2: Given a scenario, use appropriate cryptographic methods.

    REF: 9-380

57. On which standard is WPA2 based?

    A. IEEE 802.11a

    B. IEEE 802.11b

    C. IEEE 802.11g

    D. IEEE 802.11i

    Security+ SY0-401 Objective 6.2: Given a scenario, use appropriate cryptographic methods.

    REF: 9-382

58. The Extensible Authentication Protocol (EAP) was created as a secure alternative for
    _____.

    A. CHAP

    B. LEAP

    C. CCMP

    D. WPA2

    Security+ SY0-401 Objective 6.2: Given a scenario, use appropriate cryptographic methods.

    REF: 9-383

6

59. What proprietary EAP method, developed by Cisco Systems, is based on the Microsoft implementation of CHAP?
    A. CCMP
    B. PAP
    C. LEAP
    A. PEAP
    Security+ SY0-401 Objective 6.2: Given a scenario, use appropriate cryptographic methods.
    REF: 9-383

60. Which authentication protocol was designed to simplify the deployment of 802.1x by using Microsoft Windows logins and passwords?
    A. LEAP
    B. PEAP
    C. CCMP
    D. PAP
    Security+ SY0-401 Objective 6.2: Given a scenario, use appropriate cryptographic methods.
    REF: 9-383

61. Which term defines a technology used to associate a user's identity to a public key and that has been "digitally signed" by a trusted third party?
    A. Digital ID
    B. Entity ID
    C. Digital certificate
    D. Electronic passport
    Security+ SY0-401 Objective 6.3: Given a scenario, use appropriate PKI, certificate management, and associated components.
    REF: 6-231

62. Which agency is responsible for issuing digital certificates?
    A. Certificate Authority
    B. Certificate Signing Agency
    C. Registration Authority
    D. Certificate Repository
    Security+ SY0-401 Objective 6.3: Given a scenario, use appropriate PKI, certificate management, and associated components.
    REF: 6-232

63. What does a subscriber requesting a digital certificate need to do after generating the public and private keys?

    A. Publish certificate status information.

    B. Generate certificate status information.

    C. Generate a Certificate Signing Request.

    D. Revoke other public key certificates she owns.

    Security+ SY0-401 Objective 6.3: Given a scenario, use appropriate PKI, certificate management, and associated components.

    REF: 6-232

64. Which term defines a list of certificate serial numbers that have been cancelled?

    A. Certificate Expiration Notice

    B. Online Certificate Status Protocol

    C. Certificate Repository

    D. Certificate Revocation List

    Security+ SY0-401 Objective 6.3: Given a scenario, use appropriate PKI, certificate management, and associated components.

    REF: 6-234

65. What is the underlying framework for the management of public keys used in digital certificates?

    A. Certificate Repository

    B. Public Key Infrastructure

    C. Certificate Authority

    D. Online Certificate Status Protocol

    Security+ SY0-401 Objective 6.3: Given a scenario, use appropriate PKI, certificate management, and associated components.

    REF: 6-240

66. Which term signifies a numbered set of PKI standards that have been defined by the RSA Corporation?

    A. CRL

    B. PKCS

    C. OCSP

    D. PKIS

    Security+ SY0-401 Objective 6.3: Given a scenario, use appropriate PKI, certificate management, and associated components.

    REF: 6-240

6

67. Which trust model assigns a single hierarchy with one master CA called the root?

    A. Hierarchical

    B. Direct

    C. Third-party

    D. Distributed

    Security+ SY0-401 Objective 6.3: Given a scenario, use appropriate PKI, certificate management, and associated components.

    REF: 6-242

68. Which trust model has one CA that acts as a "facilitator" to interconnect all other CAs?

    A. Third-party

    B. Hierarchical

    C. Distributed

    D. Bridge

    Security+ SY0-401 Objective 6.3: Given a scenario, use appropriate PKI, certificate management, and associated components.

    REF: 6-244

69. Which key handling procedure involves splitting the private key, encrypting each half, registering the two halves, and sending the key parts to a third party for storage?

    A. Key recovery

    B. Key escrow

    C. Key integration

    D. Key delegation

    Security+ SY0-401 Objective 6.3: Given a scenario, use appropriate PKI, certificate management, and associated components.

    REF: 6-247

70. Which term defines a highly trusted person responsible for recovering lost or damaged digital certificates?

    A. Key recovery agent

    B. Key renewal agency

    C. Key escrow agent

    D. Key management agency

    Security+ SY0-401 Objective 6.3: Given a scenario, use appropriate PKI, certificate management, and associated components.

    REF: 6-247

Part II

CompTIA Security+ EXAM ANSWERS SY0-401

Domain 1.0 Network Security

Domain 2.0 Compliance and Operational Security

Domain 3.0 Threats and Vulnerabilities

Domain 4.0 Application, Data, and Host Security

Domain 5.0 Access Control and Identity Management

Domain 6.0 Cryptography

1.0

NETWORK SECURITY

Question	Answer	Explanation
1	D	Although a host-based application software firewall that runs as a program on one client is different from a hardware-based network firewall designed to protect an entire network, their functions are essentially the same: to inspect packets and either accept or deny entry.
2	A	Packets can be filtered by a firewall in one of two ways. Stateless packet filtering looks at the incoming packet and permits or denies it based on the conditions that have been set by the administrator. Stateful packet filtering keeps a record of the state of a connection between an internal computer and an external device and then makes decisions based on the connection as well as the conditions.
3	C	Traditional firewalls are rule-based while more modern firewalls are application-based.
4	D	Rule-based systems are static in nature and cannot do anything other than what they have been expressly configured to do.
5	B	A router is a network device that can forward packets across different computer networks. When a router receives an incoming packet, it reads the destination address and then, using information in its routing table, sends the packet to the next network toward its destination.
6	D	Early local area networks (LANs) used a hub, which is a standard network device for connecting multiple network devices together so that they function as a single network segment. A network switch is a device that connects network devices together. However, unlike a hub, a switch has a degree of "intelligence."
7	A	A network tap is generally best for high-speed networks that have a large volume of traffic, while port mirroring is better for networks with light traffic.

A

Question	Answer	Explanation
8	C	Because load balancers generally are located between routers and servers, they can detect and stop attacks directed at a server or application.
9	B	Load balancing that is used for distributing HTTP requests received is sometimes called IP spraying.
10	A	A proxy server is a computer or an application program that intercepts user requests from the internal secure network and then processes that request on behalf of the user.
11	D	A web security gateway can block malicious content in real time as it appears (without first knowing the URL of a dangerous site).
12	A	A virtual private network (VPN) is a technology that enables authorized users to use an unsecured public network, such as the Internet, as if it were a secure private network.
13	B	VPN transmissions are achieved through communicating with endpoints. An endpoint is the end of the tunnel between VPN devices. An endpoint can be software on a local computer, a dedicated hardware device such as a VPN concentrator (which aggregates hundreds or thousands of VPN connections), or integrated into another networking device such as a firewall.
14	C	One of the advantages of behavior-based monitoring is that it is not necessary to update signature files or compile a baseline of statistical behavior before monitoring can take place. In addition, behavior-based monitoring can more quickly stop new attacks.
15	D	A method for auditing usage is to examine network traffic, activity, transactions, or behavior and look for well-known patterns, much like antivirus scanning. This is known as signature-based monitoring because it compares activities against a predefined signature.
16	D	Anomaly-based monitoring is designed for detecting statistical anomalies.
17	B	Heuristic monitoring is founded on experience-based techniques. It attempts to answer the question, "Will this do something harmful if it is allowed to execute?"
18	A	A protocol analyzer captures packets to decode and analyzes their contents.
19	C	Installing the spam filter with the SMTP serve is the simplest and most effective approach.

Question	Answer	Explanation
20	D	Internet content filters monitor Internet traffic and block access to preselected websites and files. A requested webpage is displayed only if it complies with the specified filters. Unapproved websites can be restricted based on the Uniform Resource Locator or URL (URL filtering) or by searching for and matching keywords such as sex or hate (content inspection) as well as looking for malware (malware inspection).
21	A	With malware inspection and filtering, filters can assess if a webpage contains any malicious elements or exhibits any malicious behavior, and then flag questionable pages with a warning message.
22	D	A Web application firewall is a special type of firewall that looks at the applications using HTTP.
23	B	A more "intelligent" firewall is an application-aware firewall, sometimes called a next-generation firewall (NGFW).
24	B	One of the major differences between a NIDS and a NIPS is its location. A NIDS has sensors that monitor the traffic entering and leaving a firewall, and reports back to the central device for analysis. A NIPS, on the other hand, would be located "in line" on the firewall itself. This can allow the NIPS to more quickly take action to block an attack.
25	D	A network intrusion prevention system (NIPS) is similar to a NIDS in that it monitors network traffic to immediately react to block a malicious attack. One of the major differences between a NIDS and a NIPS is its location. A NIDS has sensors that monitor the traffic entering and leaving a firewall, and reports back to the central device for analysis. A NIPS, on the other hand, would be located "in line" on the firewall itself. This can allow the NIPS to more quickly take action to block an attack.
26	C	Firewall rules are essentially an IF-THEN construction. IF these rule conditions are met, THEN the action occurs.
27	A	The source port is the TCP/IP port number being used to send packets of data through. Options for setting the source port often include a specific port number, a range of numbers, or Any (port).
28	C	Some general principles for managing VLANs are: (1) Configure empty switch ports to connect to an unused VLAN (2) Change any default VLAN names (3) Configure the ports on the switch that pass tagged VLAN packets to explicitly forward specific tags (4) Configure VLANs so that public devices, such as a web application server, are not on a private VLAN, forcing users to have access to that VLAN.

A

Question	Answer	Explanation
29	D	The configuration of the router should be performed from the console and not a remote location. This configuration can then be stored on a secure network drive as a backup and not on a laptop or USB flash drive.
30	C	Although access control lists (ACLs) can be associated with any type of object, these lists are most often viewed in relation to files maintained by the operating system. ACLs have limitations. First, using ACLs is not efficient. Second, they can be difficult to manage in an enterprise setting where many users need to have different levels of access to many different resources. Note that the structure behind ACL tables can be complex.
31	A	Ports can be secured through disabling unused interfaces, using MAC limiting and filtering, and through IEEE 802.1x.
32	B	The IEEE 802.1x standard provides the highest degree of port security by implementing port-based authentication.
33	A	One defense against DoS and DDoS SYN flood attacks is to use a flood guard. A flood guard is a feature that controls a device's tolerance for unanswered service requests and helps to prevent a DoS attack.
34	D	Broadcast storms can be prevented with loop protection, which uses the IEEE 802.1d standard spanning-tree algorithm (STA).
35	D	Broadcast storms can be prevented with loop protection, which uses the IEEE 802.1d standard spanning-tree algorithm (STA).
36	C	Implicit deny in access control means that if a condition is not explicitly met, the request for access is rejected. (Implicit means that something is implied or indicated but not actually expressed.)
37	A	One way to provide network separation is to physically separate users by connecting them to different switches and routers. This prevents bridging and even prevents a reconfigured device from allowing that connection to occur.
38	D	A security access log can provide details regarding requests for specific files on a system while an audit log is used to record which user performed an action and what that action was. System event logs document any unsuccessful events and the most significant successful events.
39	D	Perhaps the biggest obstacle to log management is that different devices record log information in different formats and even with different data captured. Combining multiple logs, each with a different format, can be a major challenge.

Question	Answer	Explanation
40	B	An integrated device that combines several security functions, called a Unified Threat Management (UTM) security product.
41	D	In order to allow untrusted outside users access to resources such as web servers, most networks employ a demilitarized zone (DMZ). The DMZ functions as a separate network that rests outside the secure network perimeter: untrusted outside users can access the DMZ but cannot enter the secure network.
42	C	Allowing an IP address to be split anywhere within its 32 bits. This is known as subnetting or subnet addressing.
43	D	Improved addressing techniques introduced in 1985 allowed an IP address to be split anywhere within its 32 bits. This is known as subnetting or subnet addressing. Instead of just having networks and hosts, with subnetting, networks essentially can be divided into three parts: network, subnet, and host.
44	C	Networks are usually segmented by using switches to divide the network into a hierarchy.
45	B	Core switches reside at the top of the hierarchy and carry traffic between switches, while workgroup switches are connected directly to the devices on the network.
46	B	Segmenting a network by separating devices into logical groups is known as creating a virtual LAN (VLAN).
47	A	Network address translation (NAT) is a technique that allows private IP addresses to be used on the public Internet.
48	A	A variation of NAT is port address translation (PAT). Instead of giving each outgoing packet a different IP address, each packet is given the same IP address but a different TCP port number. This allows a single public IP address to be used by several users.
49	D	Remote access refers to any combination of hardware and software that enables remote users to access a local internal network.
50	A	Using Internet Protocol (IP), various services such as voice, video, and data can be combined (multiplexed) and transported under a universal format. IP telephony is using a data based IP network to add digital voice clients and new voice applications onto the IP network.
51	B	Instead of managing separate voice and data networks, convergence provides the functionality of managing and supporting a single network for all applications.

A

Question	Answer	Explanation
52	A	The goal of NAC is to prevent computers with suboptimal security from potentially infecting other computers through the network.
53	B	Virtualization is a means of managing and presenting computer resources by function without regard to their physical layout or location.
54	A	One type of virtualization in which an entire operating system environment is simulated is known as host virtualization. Instead of using a physical computer, a virtual machine, which is a simulated software-based emulation of a computer, is created. The host system (the operating system installed on the computer's hardware) runs a hypervisor that manages the virtual machine operating systems and supports one or more guest systems (a foreign virtual operating system).
55	D	Virtualization has several advantages. First, new virtual server machines can be quickly made available (host availability), and resources such as the amount of Random Access Memory (RAM) or hard drive space can easily be expanded or contracted as needed (host elasticity).
56	B	Cloud computing, which is a pay-per-use computing model in which customers pay only for the online computing resources they need, has emerged as a revolutionary concept that can dramatically impact all areas of IT, including network design, applications, procedures, and even personnel.
57	D	Unlike Software as a Service (SaaS), in which the application software belonging to the cloud computing vendor is used, in Platform as a Service (PaaS), consumers can install and run their own specialized applications on the cloud computing network.
58	C	In the Software as a Service (SaaS) model, the cloud computing vendor provides access to the vendor's software applications running on a cloud infrastructure. These applications, which can be accessed through a web browser, do not require any installation, configuration, upgrading, or management from the user.
59	D	In the Infrastructure as a Service (IaaS) model, the customer has the highest level of control. The cloud computing vendor allows customers to deploy and run their own software, including operating systems and applications. Consumers have some control over the operating systems, storage, and their installed applications, but do not manage or control the underlying cloud infrastructure.

Question	Answer	Explanation
60	C	A private cloud is created and maintained on a private network. Although this type offers the highest level of security and control (because the company must purchase and maintain all the software and hardware), it also reduces any cost savings.
61	B	A public cloud is one in which the services and infrastructure are offered to all users with access provided remotely through the Internet.
62	B	A hybrid cloud is a combination of public and private clouds.
63	A	A community cloud is a cloud that is open only to specific organizations that have common concerns.
64	D	A basic level of security can be achieved through using the security features found in standard network hardware. And because networks typically contain multiple types of network hardware, this allows for layered security, also called defense in depth.
65	C	Internet Protocol Security (IPsec) is a protocol suite for securing Internet Protocol (IP) communications.
66	D	IPsec supports two encryption modes: transport and tunnel.
67	A	The Simple Network Management Protocol (SNMP) is a popular protocol used to manage network equipment and is supported by most network equipment manufacturers.
68	C	Secure Shell (SSH) is an encrypted alternative to the Telnet protocol that is used to access remote computers.
69	C	The Domain Name System (DNS) is a TCP/IP protocol that resolves (maps) a symbolic name (www.cengage.com) with its corresponding IP address (69.32.133.11).
70	D	A newer secure version of DNS known as Domain Name System Security Extensions (DNSSEC) allows DNS information to be digitally signed so that an attacker cannot forge DNS information.
71	D	Transport Layer Security (TLS) is a cryptographic transport algorithm.
72	C	One of the most common cryptographic transport algorithms is Secure Sockets Layer (SSL). This protocol was developed by Netscape in 1994 in response to the growing concern over Internet security.

A

Question	Answer	Explanation
73	A	Computer networks also have protocols, or rules for communication. These protocols are essential for proper communication to take place between network devices. The most common protocol used today for both local area networks (LANs) and the Internet is Transmission Control Protocol/Internet Protocol (TCP/IP).
74	A	TCP/IP uses its own four-layer architecture that includes Network Interface, Internet, Transport, and Application layers.
75	B	There are several differences between SFTP and FTPS. First, FTPS is a combination of two technologies (FTP and SSL or TLS), whereas SFTP is an entire protocol itself and is not pieced together with multiple parts. Second, SFTP uses only a single TCP port instead of two ports like FTPS. Finally, SFTP encrypts and compresses all data and commands (FTPS may not encrypt data).
76	A	A weakness of FTPS is that although the control port commands are encrypted, the data port (port 20) may or may not be encrypted.
77	C	One common use of TLS and SSL is to secure Hypertext Transport Protocol (HTTP) communications between a browser and a web server. This secure version is actually "plain" HTTP sent over SSL or TLS and is called Hypertext Transport Protocol Secure (HTTPS).
78	D	Secure Copy Protocol (SCP) is used for file transfers. SCP is an enhanced version of Remote Copy Protocol (RCP). SCP encrypts files and commands.
79	D	Secure Copy Protocol (SCP) encrypts files and commands, yet has limitations. For example, a file transfer cannot be interrupted and then resumed in the same session; the session must be completely terminated and then restarted.
80	A	Different IP devices on a network often need to share between them specific information. However, IP does not have the capability for devices to exchange these low-level control messages. The communications between devices is handled by one of the core protocols of TCP/IP, namely, Internet Control Message Protocol (ICMP).
81	C	In an Internet Control Message Protocol (ICMP) redirect attack, an ICMP redirect packet is sent to the victim that asks the host to send its packets to another "router," which is actually a malicious device.
82	D	In a ping of death attack, a malformed ICMP ping that exceeds the size of an IP packet is sent to the victim's computer. This can cause the host to crash.

Question	Answer	Explanation
83	D	An Internet Protocol version 4 (IPv4) address is 32 bits in length, providing about 4.3 billion possible IP address combinations. This no longer is sufficient for the number of devices that are being connected to the Internet.
84	A	IPv6 expands the length of source and destination IP addresses from IPv4's 32 bits to 128 bits.
85	A	iSCSI (Internet Small Computer System Interface) is an IP-based storage networking standard for linking data storage facilities. Because it works over a standard IP network, iSCSI can transmit data over LANs, wide area networks (WANs), and the Internet.
86	C	Fibre Channel (FC) is a high-speed storage network protocol that can transmit up to 16 gigabits per second.
87	C	A variation of FC is Fibre Channel over Ethernet (FCoE) that encapsulates Fibre Channel frames over Ethernet networks. This allows Fibre Channel to use fast Ethernet networks while preserving the Fibre Channel protocol.
88	A	Transferring files can be performed using the File Transfer Protocol (FTP), which is an unsecure TCP/IP protocol. FTP is used to connect to an FTP server, much in the same way that HTTP links to a web server.
89	C	There are several differences between Secure FTP (SFTP) and FTP Secure (FTPS). First, FTPS is a combination of two technologies (FTP and SSL or TLS), whereas SFTP is an entire protocol itself and is not pieced together with multiple parts. Second, SFTP uses only a single TCP port instead of two ports like FTPS. Finally, SFTP encrypts and compresses all data and commands (FTPS may not encrypt data).
90	C	A "light" version of File Transfer Protocol (FTP) known as Trivial File Transfer Protocol (TFTP) uses a small amount of memory but has limited functionality. It is often used for the automated transfer of configuration files between devices.
91	A	Telnet is an older TCP/IP protocol for text-based communication. In addition, Telnet is also an application. This application is a terminal emulation program that runs on a local computer that connects to a server on the network. Commands can be entered using the Telnet application to the remote server as if the user was at the server itself.
92	B	Hypertext Transport Protocol (HTTP), which is the standard protocol for Internet usage.

A

Question	Answer	Explanation
93	A	NetBIOS (Network Basic Input/Output System) is a transport protocol used by Microsoft Windows systems to allow applications on separate computers to communicate over a LAN.
94	B	The File Transfer Protocol (FTP) uses port 21 for commands.
95	B	The Secure Shell (SSH) protocol uses port 22.
96	A	The Simple Mail Transfer Protocol (SMTP) uses port 25.
97	B	The Domain Name System (DNS) protocol uses port 53.
98	C	The Hypertext Transfer Protocol (HTTP) uses port 80.
99	D	The Post Office Protocol v3 (POP3) uses port 110.
100	B	NetBIOS uses port 139.
101	B	The Internet Message Access Protocol (IMAP) uses port 143.
102	C	The Hypertext Transfer Protocol Secure (HTTPS) uses port 443.
103	D	The Microsoft Terminal Server uses port 3389.
104	C	TCP/IP uses its own four-layer architecture that includes Network Interface, Internet, Transport, and Application layers. This corresponds generally to the OSI reference model.
105	A	There are two modes of WPA. WPA Personal was designed for individuals or small office/home office (SOHO) settings, which typically have 10 or fewer employees. A more robust WPA Enterprise was intended for larger enterprises, schools, and government agencies. WPA addresses both encryption and authentication.
106	B	WPA2 addresses the two major security areas of WLANs, namely, encryption and authentication.
107	C	Wired Equivalent Privacy (WEP) is an IEEE 802.11 security protocol designed to ensure that only authorized parties can view transmitted wireless information.
108	D	A framework for transporting the authentication protocols is known as the Extensible Authentication Protocol (EAP). EAP was created as a more secure alternative than the weak Challenge Handshake Authentication Protocol (CHAP) and Password Authentication Protocol (PAP). Despite its name, EAP is a framework for transporting authentication protocols instead of the authentication protocol itself.

Question	Answer	Explanation
109	A	Protected EAP (PEAP) is designed to simplify the deployment of 802.1x by using Microsoft Windows logins and passwords. PEAP is considered a more flexible PEAP scheme because it creates an encrypted channel between the client and the authentication server, and the channel then protects the subsequent user authentication exchange.
110	A	Lightweight EAP (LEAP) is a proprietary EAP method developed by Cisco Systems and is based on the Microsoft implementation of CHAP. It requires mutual authentication used for WLAN encryption using Cisco client software (there is no native support for LEAP in Microsoft Windows operating systems).
111	B	The most common type of wireless access control is Media Access Control (MAC) address filtering. The MAC address is a hardware address that uniquely identifies each node of a network.
112	D	The SSID can be easily discovered even when it is not contained in beacon frames because it is transmitted in other management frames sent by the AP. Attackers with protocol analyzers can still detect the SSID.
113	A	The heart and soul of WPA is a newer encryption technology called Temporal Key Integrity Protocol (TKIP). TKIP functions as a "wrapper" around WEP by adding an additional layer of security but still preserving WEP's basic functionality.
114	C	The encryption protocol used for WPA2 is the Counter Mode with Cipher Block Chaining Message Authentication Code Protocol (CCMP) and specifies the use of CCM (a general purpose cipher mode algorithm providing data privacy) with AES.
115	B	Generally the AP can be secured to the ceiling or high on a wall. It is recommended that APs be mounted as high as possible for two reasons: there may be fewer obstructions for the RF signal, and to prevent thieves from stealing the device.
116	D	A security feature on some APs is the ability to adjust the level of power at which the WLAN transmits. On devices with that feature, the power can be adjusted so that less of the signal leaves the premises and reaches outsiders.
117	A	A captive portal AP uses a standard web browser to provide information, and gives the wireless user the opportunity to agree to a policy or present valid login credentials, providing a higher degree of security.

A

Question	Answer	Explanation
118	C	Although all wireless network interface card (NIC) adapters have embedded antennas, attaching an external antenna will significantly increase the ability to detect a wireless signal.
119	B	Ensuring that a wireless LAN can provide its intended functionality and meet its required design goals can best be achieved through a site survey. A site survey is an in-depth examination and analysis of a wireless LAN site.
120	D	Software-based VPNs, often used on mobile devices like laptops in which the VPN endpoint is actually software running on the device itself, offer the most flexibility in how network traffic is managed.

2.0

COMPLIANCE AND OPERATIONAL SECURITY

Question	Answer	Explanation
1	D	Risk avoidance involves identifying the risk but making the decision to not engage in the activity.
2	C	Acceptance simply means that the risk is acknowledged but no steps are taken to address it.
3	B	Risk mitigation is the attempt to address the risks by making risk less serious.
4	A	Risk deterrence involves understanding something about the attacker and then informing him of the harm that may come his way if he attacks an asset.
5	C	Risk transference is the act of transferring the risk to a third party.
6	A	Existing security tools, such as antivirus, antispam, and IDS, were designed for single physical servers and do not always adapt well to multiple virtual machines.
7	D	In cloud computing, the customer's data must be properly isolated from that of other customers, and the highest level of application availability and security must be maintained.
8	C	Separation of duties requires that if the fraudulent application of a process could potentially result in a breach of security, the process should be divided between two or more individuals.
9	A	An advantage of job rotation is that it helps to expose any potential avenues for fraud by having multiple individuals with different perspectives learn about the job and uncover vulnerabilities that someone else may have overlooked.

A

Question	Answer	Explanation
10	A	Job rotation limits the amount of time that individuals are in a position to manipulate security configurations.
11	D	Limiting access to rooms in a building is a model of the information technology security principle of least privilege.
12	B	In many fraud schemes, the perpetrator must be present every day in order to continue the fraud or keep it from being exposed. Many organizations require mandatory vacations for all employees to counteract this.
13	A	Mean time to recovery (MTTR) is the average amount of time that it will take a device to recover from a failure that is not a terminal failure.
14	C	The term mean time between failures refers to the average (mean) amount of time until a component fails, cannot be repaired, and must be replaced.
15	B	The recovery point objective (RPO) is the maximum length of time that an organization can tolerate between backups.
16	D	The recovery time objective is the length of time it will take to recover the data that has been backed up.
17	B	An event that, in the beginning, is considered to be a risk yet turns out not to be one is called a false positive.
18	C	A false negative is an event that does not appear to be a risk but actually turns out to be one.
19	C	Management risk control types are administrative in their nature and are the laws, regulations, policies, practices, and guidelines that govern the overall requirements and controls.
20	A	Technical risk control types involve enforcing technology to control risk, such as antivirus software, firewalls, and encryption.
21	D	Operational risk control types may include using video surveillance systems and barricades to limit access to secure sites.
22	B	The qualitative approach to calculating risk uses an "educated guess" based on observation.
23	D	The quantitative approach to calculating risk attempts to create "hard" numbers associated with the risk of an element in a system by using historical data.
24	D	Mean Time To Failure (MTTF) is the average amount of time expected until the first failure of a piece of equipment.

Question	Answer	Explanation
25	D	Historical data can be used to determine the likelihood of a risk occurring within a year. This is known as the Annualized Rate of Occurrence (ARO).
26	C	The Annualized Loss Expectancy (ALE) is the expected monetary loss that can be expected for an asset due to a risk over a one-year period.
27	D	Consider a building with a value of $10,000,000 (AV) of which 75 percent of it is likely to be destroyed by a tornado (EF). The SLE would be calculated as follows: $7,500,000 = $10,000,000 x 0.75
28	B	The Single Loss Expectancy (SLE) is the expected monetary loss every time a risk occurs.
29	C	A security policy is a written document that states how an organization plans to protect the company's information technology assets.
30	A	An effective security policy must carefully balance two key elements: trust and control.
31	B	A privacy policy outlines how the organization uses personal information it collects.
32	D	An Acceptable Use Policy (AUP) is a policy that defines the actions users may perform while accessing systems and networking equipment.
33	B	On-boarding business partners refers to the start-up relationship between partners
34	A	A Service Level Agreement (SLA) is a service contract between a vendor and a client that specifies what services will be provided, the responsibilities of each party, and any guarantees of service.
35	C	A Blanket Purchase Agreement (BPA) is a prearranged purchase or sale agreement between a government agency and a business.
36	B	A Memorandum of Understanding (MOU) describes an agreement between two or more parties.
37	D	An Interconnection Security Agreement (ISA) is an agreement that is intended to minimize security risks for data transmitted across a network.
38	D	Off-boarding business partners is the termination of an agreement between parties.

A

Question	Answer	Explanation
39	C	One of the means by which the parties can reach an understanding of their relationships and responsibilities is through interoperability agreements, particularly as they relate to security policy and procedures.
40	A	Data loss prevention (DLP) is a system of security tools that is used to recognize and identify data that is critical to the organization and to ensure that it is protected.
41	A	Audits serve to verify that the organization's security protections are being enacted and that corrective actions can be swiftly implemented before an attacker exploits a vulnerability.
42	B	One element of privilege management is periodic review of a subject's privileges over an object, known as privilege auditing
43	D	Change management refers to a methodology for making modifications and keeping track of those changes.
44	C	The objective of incident management is to restore normal operations as quickly as possible with the least possible impact on either the business or the users.
45	A	If the forensics response team is external to the organization, it is important that they accurately track their hours and expenses from the start of the investigation.
46	C	Securing a crime scene involves documenting the physical surroundings of the computer with video; interviewing witnesses; and taking photographs of images displayed on the screen.
47	D	The term order of volatility is used to describe the sequence of volatile data that must be preserved in a computer forensic investigation.
48	A	Capturing this volatile information can best be performed by capturing the entire system image, which is a snapshot of the current state of the computer that contains all current settings and data.
49	B	During the process of preserving the evidence, hashing algorithms are used as part of the validation process by mirror image backup programs to ensure accuracy.
50	B	While preserving the evidence of a crime, any data such as contents of RAM, current network connections, logon sessions, network traffic and logs, and any open files must be captured and saved.
51	D	Big data analysis is conducted during the "examining the evidence" stage of forensic analysis.

Question	Answer	Explanation
52	C	A chain of custody includes documenting all of the serial numbers of the systems involved, who handled and had custody of the systems and for what length of time, how the computer was shipped, and any other steps in the process.
53	C	The chain of custody documents that the evidence was under strict control at all times and no unauthorized person was given the opportunity to corrupt the evidence.
54	B	During the execution phase of incident response, the incident must first be properly identified, and then key personnel must be notified and the procedures escalated as necessary.
55	B	During the execution phase of incident response, damage and loss control steps should be taken to mitigate damage, particularly in the event of a data breach.
56	B	During the execution phase of incident response, equipment must be isolated by either quarantine or the entire removal of the device itself.
57	A	During the analysis phase of incident response, a "lessons learned" analysis should be conducted in order to use the event to build stronger incident response policies and procedures in the future.
58	D	Organizations instruct their users that the computer forensics response team must be contacted immediately. This team serves as first responders whenever digital evidence needs to be preserved.
59	B	Compliance training involves making users aware of the organization's established security strategy as well as the reasons why it is necessary to adhere to it.
60	C	Clean desk policy requires employees to clear their workspace of all papers at the end of each business day.
61	B	Data handling instructs that no sensitive data may leave the premises without prior authorization.
62	A	Prevent tailgating instructs that you should never allow another person to enter a secure area along with you without displaying their ID card.
63	D	A P2P network does not have servers, so each device simultaneously functions as both a client and a server to all other devices connected to the network.
64	C	The most common type of P2P network is known as BitTorrent.
65	B	Grouping individuals and organizations into clusters or groups based on some sort of affiliation is called social networking.

A

Question	Answer	Explanation
66	D	Role-based training involves specialized training that is customized to the specific role that an employee holds in the organization.
67	D	A deterrent control attempts to discourage security violations before they occur.
68	A	Preventive controls work to prevent the threat from coming into contact with the vulnerability.
69	C	Administrative controls are the processes for developing and ensuring that policies and procedures are carried out.
70	C	Detective controls are designed to identify any threat that has reached the system.
71	C	The following is used to extinguish a class A fire: water, water-based chemical, foam, or multipurpose dry chemical
72	A	The following is used to extinguish a Class C fire: foam, dry chemical, or carbon dioxide to put out the fire by smothering it or cutting off the oxygen
73	D	The following is used to extinguish a Class K fire: special extinguisher converts oils to noncombustible soaps
74	B	The following is used to extinguish a Class D fire: dry powder or other special sodium extinguishing agents
75	D	A defense for shielding an electromagnetic field is a Faraday cage.
76	B	In a data center using a hot aisle/cold aisle layout, the server racks are lined up in alternating rows, with cold air intakes facing one direction and hot air exhausts facing the other direction.
77	A	Electrostatic discharge (ESD) is the sudden flow of electric current between two objects, which can destroy electronic equipment.
78	D	Fencing is usually a tall, permanent structure to keep out individuals for maintaining security.
79	A	Video surveillance uses video cameras to transmit a signal to a specific and limited set of receivers called closed circuit television (CCTV).
80	A	Barricades are most often used for directing large crowds or restricting vehicular traffic and are generally not designed to keep out individuals.
81	B	A protected distribution system (PDS) is a system of cable conduits used to protect classified information that is being transmitted between two secure areas.

Question	Answer	Explanation
82	A	Motion detection is determining an object's change in position in relation to its surroundings.
83	A	A deadbolt lock extends a solid metal bar into the door frame for extra security.
84	C	A store entry double cylinder lock includes a keyed cylinder in both the outside and inside knobs so that a key in either knob locks or unlocks both at the same time
85	D	Cipher locks are combination locks that use buttons that must be pushed in the proper sequence to open the door.
86	B	A mantrap is designed to separate a nonsecured area from a secured area.
87	C	A proximity reader is a device that detects an emitted signal in order to identify the owner.
88	B	An access list is a record or list of individuals who have permission to enter a secure area, along with the time they entered and the time they left the area.
89	B	Standard biometrics can use fingerprints or other unique characteristics of a person's face, hands, or eyes (irises and retinas) to authenticate a user.
90	A	Succession planning involves determining in advance who will be authorized to take over in the event of the incapacitation or death of key employees.
91	A	Business continuity planning and testing is the process of identifying exposure to threats, creating preventive and recovery procedures, and then testing them to determine if they are sufficient.
92	C	A business impact analysis (BIA) identifies mission-critical business functions and quantifies the impact a loss of such functions may have on the organization in terms of its operational and financial position.
93	A	A business impact analysis (BIA) typically begins by identifying threats through a risk assessment.
94	B	IT contingency planning is developing an outline of procedures that are to be followed in the event of major IT incident (a denial-of-service attack) or an incident that directly impacts IT (a building fire).
95	D	Disaster recovery involves creating, implementing, and testing disaster recovery plans. These plans typically include procedures to address redundancy and fault tolerance as well as data backups.

A

Question	Answer	Explanation
96	B	Tabletop exercises simulate an emergency situation but in an informal and stress-free environment.
97	C	The term high availability is used to describe a system that can function for an extended period of time with little downtime.
98	D	The term single point of failure is used to describe a component or entity in a system which, if it no longer functions, would adversely affect the entire system.
99	A	A server cluster is the combination of two or more servers that are interconnected to appear as one.
100	B	The term RAID is used to describe a technology that uses multiple hard disk drives for increased reliability and performance.
101	C	Load balancers can provide a degree of network redundancy by blocking traffic to servers that are not functioning.
102	C	A hot site is generally run by a commercial disaster recovery service that allows a business to continue computer and network operations to maintain business continuity.
103	D	A cold site provides office space, but the customer must provide and install all the equipment needed to continue operations.
104	A	A warm site has all the equipment installed but does not have active Internet or telecommunications facilities, and does not have current backups of data.
105	D	Two elements are used in the calculation of when data backups should be performed. These are recovery point objective and recovery time objective.
106	C	The security goal *confidentiality* involves the use of encryption, steganography, and access controls.
107	B	The security goal *integrity* involves the use of hashing, digital signatures, certificates, nonrepudiation tools.
108	D	The security goal *availability* involves the use of redundancy, fault tolerance, and patching.
109	A	The security goal *safety* involves the use of locks, CCTV, escape plans and routes, safety drills.
110	C	When defending external perimeters, most fencing is accompanied with a sign that explains the area is restricted and proper lighting so the area can be viewed after dark.

3.0

THREATS AND VULNERABILITIES

Question	Answer	Explanation
1	C	Malware is software that enters a computer system without the user's knowledge or consent and then performs an unwanted and usually harmful action.
2	A	Oligomorphic malware changes its internal code to one of a set number of predefined mutations whenever it is executed
3	B	Metamorphic malware can actually rewrite its own code and thus appears different each time it is executed.
4	D	One method of classifying the various types of malware is by using the primary trait that the malware possesses. These traits are circulation, infection, concealment, and payload capabilities.
5	B	A computer virus (virus) is malicious computer code that, like its biological counterpart, reproduces itself on the same computer.
6	C	Most viruses today go to great lengths to avoid detection; this type of virus is called an armored virus.
7	D	A worm is a malicious program that uses a computer network to replicate.
8	A	A computer Trojan horse (or just Trojan) is an executable program that masquerades as performing a benign activity but also does something malicious.
9	C	A rootkit is a set of software tools used to hide the actions or presence of other types of software.
10	A	Spyware is a general term used to describe software that secretly spies on users by collecting information without their consent.
11	D	Adware delivers advertising content in a manner that is unexpected and unwanted by the user.

A

Question	Answer	Explanation
12	B	Ransomware prevents a user's device from properly operating until a fee is paid.
13	D	A logic bomb is computer code that is typically added to a legitimate program but lies dormant until it is triggered by a specific logical event.
14	A	When hundreds, thousands, or even hundreds of thousands of zombie computers are gathered into a logical computer network, they create a botnet under the control of the attacker.
15	C	Backdoors that are installed on a computer allow the attacker to return at a later time and bypass security settings.
16	B	Phishing is sending an email or displaying a web announcement that falsely claims to be from a legitimate enterprise in an attempt to trick the user into surrendering private information.
17	A	The emails used in spear phishing are customized to the recipients, including their names and personal information, in order to make the message appear legitimate.
18	B	Known as vishing (voice phishing), an attacker calls a victim who, upon answering, hears a recorded message that pretends to be from the user's bank stating that her credit card has experienced fraudulent activity or that her bank account has had unusual activity.
19	C	Instead of asking the user to visit a fraudulent website, pharming automatically redirects the user to the fake site. This is accomplished by attackers penetrating the servers on the Internet that direct traffic or altering a file on the host computer.
20	C	Spammers have turned to image spam, which uses graphical images of text in order to circumvent text-based filters.
21	B	Attackers purchase fake sites with domain names that are spelled similarly to actual sites. This is called typo squatting or URL hijacking. A well-known site like google.com may have to deal with more than 1000 typo squatting domains.
22	A	A network denial of service (DoS) attack is a deliberate attempt to prevent authorized users from accessing a system by overwhelming that system with requests.
23	D	Called a smurf attack, an attacker broadcasts a ping request to all computers on the network but changes the address from which the request came to the victim's computer.
24	D	The impersonation of another computer or device is called spoofing.

Question	Answer	Explanation
25	B	Technology-based man-in-the-middle attacks are conducted on networks. This type of attack makes it appear that two computers are communicating with each other, when actually they are sending and receiving data with a computer between them, or the "man-in-the-middle."
26	A	A replay attack is similar to a passive man-in-the-middle attack. Whereas a passive attack sends the transmission immediately, a replay attack makes a copy of the transmission before sending it to the recipient. This copy is then used at a later time (the man-in-the-middle replays it).
27	D	An attacker can modify the MAC address in the ARP cache so that the corresponding IP address points to a different computer. This is known as ARP poisoning.
28	C	Privilege escalation is exploiting a vulnerability in software to gain access to resources that the user normally would be restricted from accessing.
29	D	In an automated brute force attack, every possible combination of letters, numbers, and characters is used to create candidate digests that are then matched against those in the stolen digest file.
30	B	A dictionary attack begins with the attacker creating digests of common dictionary words as candidates and then comparing them against those in a stolen digest file.
31	C	A rainbow table is a compressed representation of cleartext passwords that are related and organized in a sequence (called a chain).
32	A	Social engineering is a means of gathering information for an attack by relying on the weaknesses of individuals.
33	B	A social engineering attack relying on the principle of authority is directed by someone impersonating authority figure or falsely citing their authority.
34	B	A social engineering attack relying on the principle of intimidation is conducted by an attacker to frighten and coerce by threat.
35	A	A social engineering attack relying on the principle of consensus/social proof tries to influence the victim by what others do.
36	D	A social engineering attack relying on the principle of scarcity creates the feeling that something is in short supply.
37	C	A social engineering attack relying on the principle of urgency plants the idea that an immediate action is needed.

A

Question	Answer	Explanation
38	C	A social engineering attack relying on the principle of familiarity/liking creates the idea that the victim is well-known and well-received.
39	D	A social engineering attack relying on the principle of trust creates the sense of confidence between the attacker and the victim.
40	A	Social engineering impersonation means to masquerade as a real or fictitious character and then play out the role of that person on a victim.
41	B	Instead of going after the "smaller fish," whaling targets the "big fish," namely, wealthy individuals or senior executives within a business who typically would have larger sums of money in a bank account that an attacker could access if the attack is successful.
42	A	A hoax is a false warning, often contained in an email message claiming to come from the IT department.
43	C	Dumpster diving involves digging through trash receptacles to find information that can be useful in an attack.
44	D	Once an authorized person opens a secured door, virtually any number of individuals can follow behind and also enter. This is known as tailgating.
45	A	Known as shoulder surfing, it can be used in any setting in which a user "casually observes" someone entering an authorized code on a keypad.
46	C	A rogue AP is an unauthorized AP that allows an attacker to bypass many of the network security configurations and opens the network and its users to attacks.
47	D	In one type of wireless DoS attack, an attacker can intentionally flood the RF spectrum with extraneous RF signal "noise" that creates interference and prevents communications from occurring. This is called RF jamming.
48	B	Whereas a rogue AP is set up by an internal user, an evil twin is an AP that is set up by an attacker. This AP is designed to mimic an authorized AP, so a user's mobile device like a laptop or tablet will unknowingly connect to this evil twin instead. Attackers can then capture the transmissions from users to the evil twin AP.

Question	Answer	Explanation
49	D	Attackers can easily identify unprotected home wireless networks through war driving. War driving is searching for wireless signals from an automobile or on foot using a portable computing device. After the wireless signal has been detected, the next step is to document and then advertise the location of the wireless LANs for others to use.
50	A	Bluejacking is an attack that sends unsolicited messages to Bluetooth-enabled devices. Usually bluejacking involves sending text messages, but images and sounds also can be transmitted.
51	B	Bluesnarfing is an attack that accesses unauthorized information from a wireless device through a Bluetooth connection, often between cell phones and laptop computers.
52	A	After wireless signals are detected using war driving, the next step is to document and then advertise the location of the wireless LANs for others to use. Early WLAN users copied a system that hobos used during the Great Depression to indicate friendly locations. Wireless networks were identified by drawing on sidewalks or walls around the area of the network, known as war chalking.
53	B	To encrypt packets, WEP can use only a 64-bit or 128-bit number, which is made up of a 24-bit initialization vector (IV) and either a 40-bit or 104-bit default key. Even if a longer 128-bit number is used, the length of the IV still remains at 24 bits. The relatively short length of the IV limits its strength, since shorter keys are easier to break than longer keys.
54	A	One of the most common wireless attacks is intercepting and reading data (packet sniffing) that is being transmitted. An attacker can pick up the RF signal from an open or misconfigured AP and read any confidential wireless transmissions.
55	D	In a man-in-the-middle near field communication (NFC) attack, an attacker can intercept the NFC communications between devices and forge a fictitious response.
56	B	Man-in-the-middle attacks can be active or passive. In a passive attack, the attacker captures the data that is being transmitted, records it, and then sends it on to the original recipient without the attacker's presence being detected. This is called a wireless replay attack.
57	D	The heart and soul of WPA is a newer encryption technology called Temporal Key Integrity Protocol (TKIP). TKIP functions as a "wrapper" around WEP by adding an additional layer of security but still preserving WEP's basic functionality.

A

Question	Answer	Explanation
58	C	There are significant design and implementation flaws in WPS using the PIN method: (1) There is no lockout limit for entering PINs, so an attacker can make an unlimited number of PIN attempts. (2) The last PIN character is only a checksum. (3) The wireless router reports the validity of the first and second halves of the PIN separately, so essentially an attacker has to break only two short PIN values (a four-character PIN and a three-character PIN).
59	B	Turning off the SSID broadcast may prevent users from being able to freely roam from one AP coverage area to another.
60	A	MAC addresses are initially exchanged between wireless devices and the AP in an unencrypted format. An attacker using a protocol analyzer can easily see the MAC address of an approved device and then substitute it on her own device.
61	A	A cross-site scripting (XSS) attack injects scripts into a web application server to direct attacks at unsuspecting clients. XSS attacks occur when an attacker takes advantage of web applications that accept user input without validating it and then present it back to the user. An XSS attack requires a website that meets two criteria: it accepts user input without validating it, and it uses that input in a response.
62	D	SQL injection targets SQL servers by introducing malicious commands into them. By entering crafted SQL statements as user input, information from the database can be extracted or the existing data can be manipulated.
63	D	An XML injection attack is similar to an SQL injection attack; an attacker who discovers a website that does not filter input user data can inject XML tags and data into the database. A specific type of XML injection attack is an XPath injection, which attempts to exploit the XML Path Language (XPath) queries that are built from user input.
64	B	A directory traversal uses malformed input or takes advantage of a vulnerability to move from the root directory to restricted directories. Once the attacker has accessed a restricted directory, she can enter (inject) commands to execute on a server (called command injection) or view confidential files.
65	C	A buffer overflow attack occurs when a process attempts to store data in RAM beyond the boundaries of a fixed-length storage buffer. This extra data overflows into the adjacent memory locations (a buffer overflow). Because the storage buffer typically contains the "return address" memory location, an attacker can overflow the buffer with a new address pointing to the attacker's malware code.

Question	Answer	Explanation
66	D	An attacker could use an integer overflow attack to create a buffer overflow situation. If an integer overflow could be introduced during the calculations for the length of a buffer when a copy is occurring, it could result in a buffer that is too small to hold the data. An attacker could then use this to create her buffer overflow attack.
67	A	Many web application attacks (as well as other application attacks) exploit previously unknown vulnerabilities. Known as zero-day attacks, these attacks give victims no time—zero days—to defend against the attacks.
68	C	Cookies can pose both security and privacy risks. First-party cookies can be stolen and used to impersonate the user, while third-party cookies can be used to track the browsing or buying habits of a user.
69	C	Malicious attachments are commonly used to spread viruses, Trojans, and other malware when they are opened. Most users are unaware of the danger of attachments and routinely open any email attachment that they receive, even if it is from an unknown sender.
70	D	A locally shared object (LSO) is also called a Flash cookie, named after the Adobe Flash player. These cookies are significantly different from regular cookies in that they can store data more complex than the simple text that is typically found in a regular cookie. By default, LSOs can store up to 100 KB of data from a website, about 25 times as much as a regular cookie.
71	D	A weakness of LDAP is that it can be subject to LDAP injection attacks. These attacks, similar to SQL injection attacks, can occur when user input is not properly filtered. This may allow an attacker to construct LDAP statements based on user input statements. The attacker could then retrieve information from the LDAP database or modify its content. The defense against LDAP injection attacks is to examine all user input before processing.
72	B	One way in which malicious add-ons can be written is by using Microsoft's ActiveX. Attackers can take advantage of vulnerabilities in ActiveX to perform malicious attacks on a computer.
73	A	Session hijacking is an attack in which an attacker attempts to impersonate the user by using her session token.

A

Question	Answer	Explanation
74	A	One of the most common HTTP header manipulation attacks is response splitting. First, the application on the client computer must allow input that contains carriage return (CR) and line feed (LF) characters in the header. By inserting a CRLF in an HTTP header, these characters can not only give attackers control of the remaining HTTP headers and body of the response but also allow them to create additional responses via HTTP headers that are entirely under their control.
75	B	Unlike a buffer overflow, a heap spray is targeted and inserts data only in certain parts of memory. A heap spray is often used in an arbitrary/remote code execution attack.
76	B	Once the security policy has been created, a security baseline for the host is established. A baseline is the standard or checklist against which systems can be evaluated and audited for their level of security (security posture).
77	C	A typical operating system configuration baseline would include changing any default settings that are insecure (such as allowing Guest accounts); eliminating any unnecessary software, services, or protocols (like removing games); and enabling system security features (such as turning on the firewall).
78	A	The OS hardening technique called kernel pruning consists of removing all unnecessary features that may compromise an operating system.
79	D	In a MAC flooding attack, an attacker can overflow the switch's address table with fake MAC addresses, forcing it to act like a hub. An appropriate defense mechanism is to use a switch that can close ports with too many MAC addresses.
80	D	Instead of creating a virtual environment in which to test a threat, IDS heuristic monitoring uses an algorithm to determine if a threat exists. Heuristic monitoring can trap an application that attempts to scan ports that the other methods may not catch. With this technique, the IDS can be triggered if any application tries to scan multiple ports.
81	D	Network device logs can be very valuable in maintaining a secure defense system. For example, a firewall log can allow us to find source-routed packets.
82	A	A switch or router without port security allows attackers to connect to unused ports to access the network.
83	D	IEEE 802.1x prevents an unauthenticated device from receiving any network traffic until its identity can be verified.

Question	Answer	Explanation
84	A	When guards actively monitor a CCTV, it becomes a preventive control: any unauthorized activity seen on video surveillance will result in the guard taking immediate action by either going to the scene or calling for assistance.
85	D	Attack trees help list the types of attacks that can occur and trace how and from where the attacks may originate.
86	B	To determine our current weaknesses that might expose our assets to threats, the vulnerability appraisal process takes a snapshot of the current security of the organization.
87	B	Encryption, steganography and access controls are common controls that are important to meet confidentiality security goals.
88	B	A fail-safe control puts the system on the highest level of security.
89	A	Types of hardening techniques include: (1) Protecting accounts with passwords. (2) Disabling any unnecessary accounts. (3) Disabling all unnecessary services. (4) Protecting management interfaces and applications.
90	C	A security posture may be considered as an approach, philosophy, or strategy regarding security. A healthy security posture results from a sound and workable strategy toward managing risks.
91	D	When performing a vulnerability assessment, port scanner software can be used to search a system for port vulnerabilities.
92	B	Port scanners, such as the RADMIN port scanner, are typically used to determine the state of a port to know what applications/services are running.
93	C	A banner is a message that a service transmits when another program connects to it. When a program is used to intentionally gather this information, the process is called banner grabbing.
94	B	A protocol analyzer is hardware or software that captures packets to decode and analyze their contents.
95	D	Protocol analyzers are widely used by network administrators for network monitoring. They can assist in network troubleshooting by detecting and diagnosing network problems such as addressing errors and protocol configuration mistakes.
96	A	A vulnerability scanner is a generic term for a range of products that look for vulnerabilities in networks or systems. Vulnerability scanners for organizations are intended to identify vulnerabilities and alert network administrators to these problems. Most vulnerability scanners maintain a database that categorizes and describes the vulnerabilities that it can detect.

A

Question	Answer	Explanation
97	C	OVAL is a "common language" for the exchange of information regarding security vulnerabilities. These vulnerabilities are identified using industry-standard tools. OVAL vulnerability definitions are recorded in Extensible Markup Language (XML) and queries are accessed using the database language Structured Query Language (SQL).
98	A	A honeypot is a computer typically located in an area with limited security and loaded with software and data files that appear to be authentic, but are actually imitations of real data files.
99	B	Similar to a honeypot, a honeynet is a network set up with intentional vulnerabilities. Its purpose is also to invite attacks so that the attacker's methods can be studied and that information can be used to increase network security.
100	D	The goal of threat modeling is to better understand who the attackers are, why they attack, and what types of attacks might occur.
101	A	An attack tree provides a visual image of the attacks that could occur against an asset.
102	A	A risk assessment involves determining the damage that would result from an attack and the likelihood that the vulnerability is a risk to the organization.
103	B	Architectural design review is the process of defining a collection of hardware and software components along with their interfaces in order to create the framework for software development.
104	B	While the code is being written it is being analyzed by a code review. Presenting the code to multiple reviewers in order to reach agreement about its security can have a significant impact on reducing security vulnerabilities.
105	D	The attack surface for software is the code that can be executed by unauthorized users.
106	C	As its name implies, a vulnerability scan is an automated software search (scan) through a system for any known security weaknesses (vulnerabilities) that creates a report of those potential exposures.
107	D	A vulnerability scan examines the current security in a passive method of testing security controls.
108	C	Vulnerability scans are usually performed from inside the security perimeter and are not intended to disrupt the normal operations of the network or devices.

Question	Answer	Explanation
109	B	An intrusive vulnerability scan attempts to actually penetrate the system in order to perform a simulated attack.
110	A	A non-intrusive vulnerability scan uses only available information to hypothesize the status of the vulnerability.
111	D	Some intrusive vulnerability scanners permit the username and password (credentials) of an active account to be stored and used by the scanner, which allows the scanner to test for additional internal vulnerabilities if an attacker were able to successfully penetrate the system. This is called a credentialed vulnerability scan.
112	C	Unlike a vulnerability scan, penetration testing (pentesting) is designed to actually exploit any weaknesses in systems that are vulnerable.
113	A	Instead of using automated software, penetration testing relies upon the skill, knowledge, and cunning of the tester.
114	C	"White hat hackers" or "ethical attackers," have the organization's permission to exploit vulnerabilities in a system and then privately provide information back to that organization.
115	B	The goals of a penetration test are to actively test all security controls and, when possible, bypass those controls, verify that a threat exists, and exploit any vulnerabilities.
116	D	Whereas vulnerability scan software may uncover a vulnerability, it provides no indication regarding the risk to that specific organization.
117	B	In a black box test, the tester has no prior knowledge of the network infrastructure that is being tested. The tester must determine the location and types of systems and devices before starting the actual tests. This technique most closely mimics an attack from outside the organization.
118	D	The opposite of a black box test is a white box test.
119	C	In a white box test the tester has an in-depth knowledge of the network and systems being tested, including network diagrams, IP addresses, and even the source code of custom applications.
120	A	Between a black box test and a white box test is a gray box test, in which some limited information has been provided to the tester.

A

4.0

APPLICATION, DATA, AND HOST SECURITY

Question	Answer	Explanation
1	A	Fuzzing or fuzz testing is a software testing technique that deliberately provides invalid, unexpected, or random data as inputs to a computer program. The program is then monitored to ensure that all errors are trapped. Fuzzing, which is usually done through automated programs, is commonly used to test for security problems in software or computer systems.
2	D	One of the important steps in developing secure applications is to account for errors (also called exceptions), which are faults in a program that occur while the application is running.
3	D	One specific type of error handling is verifying responses that the user makes to the application. Although these responses could cause the program to abort, they also can be used to inject commands.
4	A	One specific type of error handling is verifying responses that the user makes to the application. Improper verification is the cause of several types of attacks, such as cross-site scripting (XSS), SQL injection, and XML injection.
5	C	To prevent cross-site scripting, the program should trap for user responses. A preferred method for trapping user responses is escaping (output encoding). This technique is used to ensure that characters are treated as data, not as characters that are relevant to the application (such as SQL).
6	D	Application development security involves application configuration baselines and secure coding concepts.

A

Question	Answer	Explanation
7	A	Application hardening is intended to prevent attackers from exploiting vulnerabilities in software applications. In application software these vulnerabilities are often exposed by a failure to properly check the input data entering into the application.
8	B	Until recently, application patch management was rare. Because few software companies had implemented patch management systems to deliver updates, users generally were left "in the dark" regarding application software patches or where to acquire them. And it was not always clear that a new version of software addressed a vulnerability or just contained new features. However, more application patch management systems are being developed to patch vulnerabilities.
9	B	Instead of input validation, a more drastic approach to preventing SQL injection attacks is to avoid using SQL relational databases altogether. As an alternative, new nonrelational databases that are better tuned for accessing large data sets, known as NoSQL, may be used. The hot debate over which database technology is better is often referred to as the NoSQL databases vs. SQL database argument.
10	C	Whereas input validation generally uses the server to perform the validation (server-side validation), it is possible to have the client perform the validation (client-side validation). In client-side validation all input validations and error recovery procedures are performed by the user's web browser. Although this method does not require server-side scripting, nevertheless it is possible for users to alter or even bypass completely the client-side validation.
11	C	Full device encryption can be enabled to apply protection to all data stored on the device.
12	A	If a lost or stolen device cannot be located, it may be necessary to perform remote wiping, which will erase sensitive data stored on the mobile device. This ensures that even if a thief is able to access the device, no sensitive data will be compromised.
13	D	With remote lockout, the mobile device can be remotely locked and a custom message sent that is displayed on the login screen.
14	C	A lock screen prevents the mobile device from being used until the user enters the correct passcode such as a PIN or password. Lock screens should be configured so that whenever the device is turned on or is left idle for a period of time, the user must enter the passcode.

Question	Answer	Explanation
15	A	Geo-fencing involves using a mobile device's GPS to define geographical boundaries where an app can be used.
16	C	Whereas mobile device management (MDM) focuses on the device, mobile application management (MAM), also called application control, comprises the tools and services responsible for distributing and controlling access to apps. These apps can be internally developed or commercially available apps.
17	D	Mobile device management (MDM) can facilitate asset tracking, or maintaining an accurate record of company owned mobile devices, as well as inventory control, which is the operation of stockrooms where mobile devices are stored prior to their dispersal to employees.
18	A	Mobile device management (MDM) can facilitate asset tracking, or maintaining an accurate record of company owned mobile devices, as well as inventory control, which is the operation of stockrooms where mobile devices are stored prior to their dispersal to employees.
19	B	Mobile device management (MDM) tools allow a device to be managed remotely by an organization. Typically MDM involves a server component, which sends out management commands to the mobile devices, and a client component, which runs on the mobile device to receive and implement the management commands. An administrator can then perform over the air (OTA) updates or configuration changes to one device, groups of devices, or all devices.
20	A	Mobile devices include a wide variety of features for the user's convenience. However, each of these can also serve as a threat vector. It is important to disable unused features and turn off those that do not support the business use of the phone or that are rarely used. One of the features that should be disabled if it is not being regularly used is Bluetooth wireless data communication in order to prevent bluejacking and bluesnarfing.
21	A	Many mobile device management tools allow users to store usernames and passwords within the device itself. Known as credential management, it serves as a "vault" for storing valuable authentication information. In addition, cryptographic keys can be stored and managed on the device.
22	D	Many mobile device management tools allow users to store usernames and passwords within the device itself. Known as credential management it serves as a "vault" for storing valuable authentication information.

A

Question	Answer	Explanation
23	D	Many users are eager to accept the flexibility of BYOD because of the following benefits: choice of device, choice of carrier, convenience and attraction.
24	D	Geo-fencing requires the app to support geo-tagging, which is adding geographical identification data.
25	D	Mobile devices that contain both personal and corporate data may separate data storage into "containers" and encrypt only the sensitive data. This "containerization" also helps companies avoid data ownership privacy issues and legal concerns regarding a user's personal data stored in a BYOD setting.
26	C	In addition to securing the mobile device, the apps on the device also should be secured. Mobile device management (MDM) tools can support application whitelisting, which ensures that only preapproved apps can run on the device.
27	A	Transitive trust is a two-way relationship that is automatically created between parent and child domains in a Microsoft Active Directory Forest. When a new domain is created, it shares resources with its parent domain by default, which can enable an authenticated user to access resources in both the child and the parent.
28	A	An option on mobile devices that contain both personal and corporate data is separating data storage into "containers" and encrypting only the sensitive data. This "containerization" also helps companies avoid data ownership privacy issues and legal concerns regarding a user's personal data stored in a BYOD setting.
29	C	To address the vulnerabilities in operating systems that are uncovered after the software has been released, software vendors usually deploy a software "fix." A fix can come in a variety of formats. A security patch is a publicly released software security update intended to repair a vulnerability; a patch is universal for all customers.
30	B	Forensics, also known as forensic science, is the application of science to questions that are of interest to the legal profession. As computers are the foundation for communicating and recording information, a new area known as computer forensics, which uses technology to search for computer evidence of a crime, can attempt to retrieve information - even if it has been altered or erased - that can be used in the pursuit of the attacker or criminal.
31	A	Off-boarding is the ability to quickly remove devices from the organization's network.

Question	Answer	Explanation
32	D	On-boarding is the ability to rapidly enroll new mobile devices.
33	C	A benefit of implementing BYOD is a simplified IT infrastructure. By using BYOD, companies do not have to support a remote data network for employees.
34	D	An Acceptable Use Policy (AUP) is a policy that defines the actions users may perform while accessing systems and networking equipment. The users are not limited to employees; the term can also include vendors, contractors, or visitors, each with different privileges. AUPs typically cover all computer use, including mobile devices.
35	B	Several changes may be performed through OS hardening to create a trusted OS. Reducing capabilities significantly restrict what resources can be accessed and by whom.
36	C	Several changes may be performed through OS hardening to create a trusted OS. Kernel pruning removes all unnecessary features that may compromise an operating system.
37	B	Antivirus software can examine a computer for any infections as well as monitor computer activity and scan new documents that might contain a virus (this scanning is typically performed when files are opened, created, or closed). If a virus is detected, options generally include cleaning the file of the virus, quarantining the infected file, or deleting the file.
38	D	With Bayesian filtering, spam filtering software analyzes every word in an email and determines how frequently a word occurs in order to determine if it is spam.
39	B	As a separate program, popup blockers are often part of a package known as antispyware that helps prevent computers from becoming infected by different types of spyware. Antivirus and antispyware software share many similarities: they must be regularly updated to defend against the most recent attacks; they can be set to both provide continuous, real-time monitoring as well as perform a complete scan of the entire computer system at one time; and they may trap different types of malware.
40	D	A popup is a small web browser window that appears over a webpage. Most popup windows are created by advertisers and launch as soon as a new website is visited. A popup blocker is a separate program or a feature incorporated within a browser that stops popup advertisements from appearing.

A

Question	Answer	Explanation
41	C	To address the vulnerabilities in operating systems that are uncovered after the software has been released, software vendors usually deploy a software "fix." A fix can come in a variety of formats. A security patch is a publicly released software security update intended to repair a vulnerability; a patch is universal for all customers. A hotfix is a software update that addresses a specific customer issue and often may not be distributed outside that customer's organization. A service pack is software that is a cumulative package of all patches and hotfixes as well as additional features.
42	D	In addition to securing the mobile device, the apps on the device also should be secured. Mobile device management (MDM) tools can support application whitelisting, which ensures that only preapproved apps can run on the device.
43	C	Instead of managing the different security options on an operating system that has been deployed, in some cases it is necessary to tighten security during the design and coding of the OS. This is called OS hardening. An operating system that has been designed in this way to be secure is a trusted OS.
44	B	Modern operating systems include a host-based application firewall that runs as a program on a local system to protect it. These firewalls are application-based.
45	B	A host-based intrusion detection system (HIDS) is a software-based application that runs on a local host computer that can detect an attack as it occurs. A HIDS is installed on each system, such as a server or desktop, that needs to be protected. A HIDS relies on agents installed directly on the system being protected. These agents work closely with the operating system, monitoring and intercepting requests in order to prevent attacks.
46	C	A cable lock can be inserted into the security slot of a portable device and rotated so that the cable lock is secured to the device, while a cable connected to the lock can then be secured to a desk or chair.
47	A	When storing a laptop, it can be placed in a safe or a locking cabinet, which is a ruggedized steel box with a lock.
48	D	When storing a laptop, it can be placed in a safe or a locking cabinet, which is a ruggedized steel box with a lock.
49	A	A host baseline for the operating system is configuration settings that will be used for each computer in the organization. Whereas the security policy determines what must be protected, the baselines are the OS settings that impose how the policy will be enforced.

Question	Answer	Explanation
50	A	Virtualization is a means of managing and presenting computer resources by function without regard to their physical layout or location. For example, computer storage devices on a SAN can be virtualized so that multiple physical storage devices can be viewed as a single logical unit.
51	C	A snapshot refers to an instance of a particular state of a virtual machine that can be saved for later use.
52	B	Patch compatibility refers to the impact of a patch on other software or even hardware.
53	A	Host availability refers to the ability to quickly make new virtual server machines available.
54	C	Host elasticity refers to the ability to easily expand or contract resources in a virtualized environment.
55	D	Testing the existing security configuration, known as security control testing, can be performed using a simulated network environment on a computer using multiple virtual machines.
56	B	A virtual machine can be used to test for potential malware. A suspicious program can be loaded into an isolated virtual machine and executed (sandboxing). If the program is malware, it will impact only the virtual machine, and it can easily be erased and a snapshot reinstalled.
57	C	Despite its impact on IT, cloud computing raises significant security concerns. It is important that the cloud provider guarantee that the means are in place by which authorized users are given access while imposters are denied. Also, all transmissions to and from "the cloud" must be adequately protected. Finally, the customer's data must be properly isolated from that of other customers, and the highest level of application availability and security must be maintained.
58	C	It is important that not only SAN data storage but also the storage network protocols be secured. An iSCSI network should be designed so that the SAN cannot be directly accessed by clients. Instead, a SAN should have its own dedicated switch that is inaccessible from clients. Fibre Channel has several security mechanisms built-in, one of which is FC zones.
59	D	Big Data refers to a collection of data sets so large and complex that it becomes difficult to process using on-hand database management tools or traditional data processing applications. How can all of this data flowing in and out of the organization be protected so that it does not fall into the wrong hands?

A

Question	Answer	Explanation
60	A	Cryptography can be applied to entire disks. This is known as whole disk encryption and protects all data on a hard drive. One example of whole disk encryption software is that included in Microsoft Windows known as BitLocker drive encryption software. BitLocker encrypts the entire system volume, including the Windows Registry and any temporary files that might hold confidential information.
61	A	Cryptography should be used to secure any and all data that needs to be protected. This includes individual files, databases, removable media, or data on mobile devices. Cryptography can be applied through either software or hardware.
62	D	Protecting individual files or multiple files through file system cryptography can be performed using software such as Pretty Good Privacy and Microsoft Windows Encrypting File System.
63	D	GNU Privacy Guard (GPG) is an open-source product. GPG versions run on Windows, UNIX, and Linux operating systems. Messages encrypted by PGP can generally be decrypted by GPG and vice versa.
64	B	Microsoft's Encrypting File System (EFS) is a cryptography system for Windows operating systems that use the Windows NTFS file system. Because EFS is tightly integrated with the file system, file encryption and decryption are transparent to the user.
65	C	The Trusted Platform Module (TPM) is essentially a chip on the motherboard of the computer that provides cryptographic services. Because all of this is done in hardware and not through the software of the operating system, malicious software cannot attack it. Also, TPM can measure and test key components as the computer is starting up. It will prevent the computer from booting if system files or data have been altered. With TPM, if the hard drive is moved to a different computer, the user must enter a recovery password before gaining access to the system volume.
66	D	A Hardware Security Module (HSM) is a secure cryptographic processor. An HSM includes an onboard key generator and key storage facility, as well as accelerated symmetric and asymmetric encryption, and can even back up sensitive material in encrypted form. Most HSMs are LAN-based appliances that can provide services to multiple devices.

Question	Answer	Explanation
67	A	Encrypted hardware-based USB devices resemble standard USB flash drives, with several significant differences: • Encrypted hardware-based USB drives will not connect to a computer until the correct password has been provided. • All data copied to the USB flash drive is automatically encrypted. • The external cases are designed to be tamper-resistant so attackers cannot disassemble the drives. • Administrators can remotely control and track activity on the devices. • Compromised or stolen drives can be remotely disabled
68	C	Self-encrypting hard disk drives (HDDs) can protect all files stored on them. When the computer or other device with a self-encrypting HDD is initially powered up, the drive and the host device perform an authentication process. If the authentication process fails, the drive can be configured to simply deny any access to the drive or even perform a "cryptographic erase" on specified blocks of data (a cryptographic erase deletes the decryption keys so that all data is permanently encrypted and unreadable). This also makes it impossible to install the drive on another computer to read its contents.
69	C	Actions that transmit the data across a network, like an email sent across the Internet, are called data in-transit.
70	D	Data at-rest is data that is stored on electronic media.
71	D	Data in-use is data actions being performed by "endpoint devices," such as creating a report from a desktop computer.
72	B	An access control list (ACL) is a set of permissions that is attached to an object. This list specifies which subjects are allowed to access the object and what operations they can perform on it. When a subject requests to perform an operation on an object, the system checks the ACL for an approved entry in order to decide if the operation is allowed.
73	C	Information that should have been deleted from hard drives often is still available on recycled computers. This is because operating systems do not always completely delete files to make the information irretrievable. Even reformatting a drive may not fully erase all of the data on it. In order to address this problem, a data wiping and disposing policy outlines the disposal of resources that are considered confidential.

A

Question	Answer	Explanation
74	A	Data policies are important because they address the different aspects of how data should be handled within an organization. These policies are particularly important for mobile devices, since their portable nature more easily exposes data to theft. A data wiping and disposing policy addresses how and when data will ultimately be erased.
75	B	Data policies are important because they address the different aspects of how data should be handled within an organization. These policies are particularly important for mobile devices, since their portable nature more easily exposes data to theft. A data retention policy outlines how to maintain information in the user's possession for a predetermined length of time.
76	B	Data policies are important because they address the different aspects of how data should be handled within an organization. These policies are particularly important for mobile devices, since their portable nature more easily exposes data to theft. One type of data policy is a data storage policy. This is a set of procedures designed to control and manage data within the organization by specifying data collection and storage.
77	C	Large-scale industrial-control systems are called SCADA (supervisory control and data acquisition). SCADA can be found in military installations, oil pipeline control systems, manufacturing environments, and nuclear power plants. These systems are increasingly becoming the targets of attackers, often because they lack basic security features.
78	A	Whereas a general-purpose personal computer is designed to be flexible and meet a wide range of user needs, an embedded system is a computer system with a dedicated function within a larger electrical or mechanical system. The operating systems of these embedded systems often are stripped-down versions of general-purpose operating systems and may contain many of the same vulnerabilities.
79	C	The two most popular versions of smartphone operating systems are Google's Android and Apple's iOS. Like other operating systems, these smartphone operating systems have vulnerabilities that attackers can exploit.
80	B	The two most popular versions of smartphone operating systems are Google's Android and Apple's iOS. Like other operating systems, these smartphone operating systems have vulnerabilities that attackers can exploit.

Question	Answer	Explanation
81	B	Very large computing systems that have significant processing capabilities are called mainframe systems. These types of systems were first introduced more than 60 years ago. Because of their high cost they are not replaced frequently. The operating systems of older mainframes may lack the ability to be updated in a timely fashion by the vendor.
82	A	Like embedded systems, many consumer game consoles contain adaptations of general-purpose operating systems and may contain some of the same vulnerabilities. The increase in network-based online gaming has provided an opening for these devices to be exploited. However, it also allows their operating systems to be regularly patched by the vendors.
83	A	In-vehicle computer systems. As automobiles become more sophisticated, the number of functions that are controlled by microprocessors continues to increase. Researchers have demonstrated that these in-vehicle computer systems often can be easily manipulated. All cars since 1996 have an On-Board Diagnostics II (OBD-II) connector that is used for troubleshooting. An attacker could plug into the OBD-II connector and change specific vehicle emission settings or erase information captured in an accident that showed the driver was at fault.
84	C	There are several basic defense methods against attacks directed toward devices in static environments. To implement network segmentation, one should keep devices on their own network separated from the regular network.
85	D	There are several basic defense methods against attacks directed toward devices in static environments. To implement security layers, one should build security in layers around the device.
86	D	There are several basic defense methods against attacks directed toward devices in static environments. To implement application firewalls, one should when feasible, install application firewalls on the device's operating system.
87	B	There are several basic defense methods against attacks directed toward devices in static environments. To implement manual updates, one should provide a means for manual software updates when automated updates cannot be used.
88	B	There are several basic defense methods against attacks directed toward devices in static environments. To implement firmware version control, one should develop a policy that keeps track of updates to firmware.

A

Question	Answer	Explanation
89	A	There are several basic defense methods against attacks directed toward devices in static environments. To implement wrappers, one should write error-checking routines that act as a substitute for a regular function that is used in testing.
90	C	There are several basic defense methods against attacks directed toward devices in static environments. To implement control redundancy and diversity, one should keep the operating system code as basic as possible to limit overlapping or unnecessary features.

5.0

ACCESS CONTROL AND
IDENTITY MANAGEMENT

Question	Answer	Explanation
1	C	RADIUS was originally designed for remote dial-in access to a corporate network.
2	B	During a RADIUS authentication with a wireless device, a wireless device, called the supplicant (it makes an "appeal" for access), sends a request to an AP requesting permission to join the WLAN.
3	A	Kerberos is an authentication system developed by the Massachusetts Institute of Technology (MIT) in the 1980s and used to verify the identity of networked users.
4	A	Kerberos tickets are difficult to copy (because they are encrypted), contain specific user information, restrict what a user can do, and expire after a few hours or a day.
5	D	Terminal Access Control Access Control System is an authentication service commonly used on UNIX devices that communicates by forwarding user authentication information to a centralized server.
6	B	A directory service is a database stored on the network itself that contains information about users and network devices.
7	C	The directory service known as X.500 has the capability to look up information by name (a white-pages service) and to browse and search for information by category (a yellow-pages service).
8	A	An LDAP injection attack is an attack that constructs LDAP statements based on user input statements, allowing the attacker to retrieve information from the LDAP database or modify its content.
9	D	LDAP traffic can be made secure by using Secure Sockets Layer (SSL) or Transport Layer Security (TLS). This is known as Secure LDAP.

A

Question	Answer	Explanation
10	B	Security Assertion Markup Language (SAML) is an Extensible Markup Language (XML) standard that allows secure web domains to exchange user authentication and authorization data.
11	D	The term access control is used to describe the mechanism used in an information system for granting or denying approval to use specific resources.
12	B	Discretionary Access Control is the least restrictive access control model in which the owner of the object has total control over it.
13	C	One of the weaknesses of Discretionary Access Control is that a subject's permissions can be "inherited" by any program that the subject executes.
14	A	Mandatory Access Control assigns users' access controls strictly according to the custodian's desires.
15	D	In a system using Mandatory Access Control, every entity (laptops, files, projects, and so on) is an object and is assigned a classification label.
16	A	Microsoft Windows' Mandatory Integrity Control ensures data integrity by controlling access to securable objects.
17	C	Role Based Access Control is a "real-world" access control model in which access is based on a user's job function within the organization.
18	D	Rule Based Access Control is an access control model that can dynamically assign roles to subjects based on a set of rules defined by a custodian.
19	D	Rule Based Access Control is often used for managing user access to one or more systems, where business changes may trigger the application of the rules that specify access changes.
20	B	Separation of duties requires that if the fraudulent application of a process could potentially result in a breach of security, the process should be divided between two or more individuals.
21	A	Least privilege in access control means that only the minimum amount of privileges necessary to perform a job or function should be allocated.
22	C	In access control, the term implicit deny means that if a condition is not explicitly met, the request for access is rejected.
23	D	An access control list is a set of permissions that is attached to an object.

Question	Answer	Explanation
24	B	In Windows, the access control entry (ACE) includes an SID, a unique number issued to the user, group, or session that is used to identify the user in all subsequent interactions with Windows security.
25	D	In Windows, the access control entry (ACE) includes an access mask, a value that specifies the rights that are allowed or denied, and is also used to request access rights when an object is opened.
26	B	In Windows, the access control entry (ACE) includes a flag that indicates the type of ACE.
27	A	Time-of-day restrictions can be used to limit when a user can log in to a system or access resources.
28	B	The term multifactor authentication is used to describe the use of more than one type of authentication credential.
29	C	The term token is used to describe a small device that can be affixed to a keychain with a window display that shows a code to be used for authentication.
30	C	A one-time password (OTP) is an authentication code that can be used only once or for a limited period of time.
31	A	The term time-based one-time password (TOTP) is used to describe a one-time password that changes after a set period of time.
32	D	HMAC-based one-time password (HOTP) is an "event-driven" one-time password that changes when a specific event occurs, such as when a user enters a personal identification number (PIN) on the token's keypad, which triggers the token to create a random code.
33	B	A common access card (CAC) is a U.S. Department of Defense (DoD) smart card that is used for identification of active-duty and reserve military personnel along with civilian employees and special contractors.
34	C	The smart card standard covering all U.S. government employees is the Personal Identity Verification (PIV).
35	A	A smart card is a card that contains an integrated circuit chip that can hold information, which can then be used as part of the authentication process.
36	D	The term single sign-on is used to describe the use of one authentication credential to access multiple accounts or applications.
37	A	OpenID is a decentralized open-source FIM that does not require specific software to be installed on the desktop.

A

Question	Answer	Explanation
38	B	The open source service OAuth permits users to share resources stored on one site with a second site without forwarding their authentication credentials to the other site.
39	D	Token credentials include a token identifier, which is a unique, random string of characters that is encrypted to protect the token from being used by unauthorized parties.
40	C	Transitive trust is a two-way relationship that is automatically created between parent and child domains in a Microsoft Active Directory Forest.
41	C	The term authentication factors is used to describe the five elements that can prove the genuineness of a user: what you know, what you have, what you are, what you do, and where you are.
42	B	A password is a secret combination of letters, numbers, and/or characters that only the user should have knowledge of.
43	C	Social engineering attacks include phishing, shoulder surfing, and dumpster diving.
44	A	With offline cracking, attackers steal the file of password digests and then load that file onto their own computers so that they can attempt to discover the passwords by comparing the stolen digest passwords with candidate digests that they have created.
45	D	In an automated brute force attack, every possible combination of letters, numbers, and characters is used to create candidate digests that are then matched against those in the stolen digest file.
46	B	A dictionary attack that uses a set of dictionary words and compares it with the stolen digests is known as a pre-image attack, in that one known digest (dictionary word) is compared to an unknown digest (stolen digest).
47	A	A hybrid attack combines a dictionary attack with a brute force attack and will slightly alter dictionary words by adding numbers to the end of the password, spelling words backward, slightly misspelling words, or including special characters such as @, $, !, or %.
48	D	Rainbow tables make password attacks easier by creating a large pregenerated data set of candidate digests.
49	A	The LAN Manager hash uses a cryptographic one-way function (OWF): instead of encrypting the password with another key, the password itself is the key.

Question	Answer	Explanation
50	B	The term key stretching describes a password hashing algorithm that requires significantly more time than standard hashing algorithms to create the digest.
51	D	The term salt is used to describe a random string that is used in hash algorithms.
52	C	Salts make dictionary attacks and brute force attacks for cracking large number of passwords much slower and limits the impact of rainbow tables.
53	C	Two popular key stretching password hash algorithms are bcrypt and PBKDF2.
54	D	Fingerprint scanners have become the most common type of standard biometric device.
55	A	Keystroke dynamics uses two unique typing variables: dwell time and flight time.
56	C	The term geolocation describes the use of technology to identify the location of a person or object using technology.
57	B	Federated identity management is a single sign-on for networks owned by different organizations.
58	D	Single sign-on holds the promise of reducing the number of usernames and passwords that users must memorize (potentially, to just one).
59	B	OpenID is a decentralized open-source FIM that does not require specific software to be installed on the desktop. It is a Uniform Resource Locator (URL)–based identity system.
60	C	Open Authorization relies on token credentials.
61	A	Challenge-Handshake Authentication Protocol is a weak authentication protocol that has been replaced by the Extensible Authentication Protocol (EAP).
62	C	Lightweight EAP is a proprietary EAP method developed by Cisco Systems and is based on the Microsoft implementation of CHAP.
63	A	Protected EAP creates an encrypted channel between the client and the authentication server. The channel then protects the subsequent user authentication exchange.
64	B	EAP-FAST securely tunnels any credential form for authentication (such as a password or a token) using TLS.

A

Question	Answer	Explanation
65	D	EAP-SIM is based on the subscriber identity module card installed in mobile phones and other devices that use Global System for Mobile Communications (GSM) networks?
66	A	The term Group Policy is used to describe a Microsoft Windows feature that provides centralized management and configuration of computers and remote users using the Microsoft directory services Active Directory (AD).
67	A	Group Policy is usually used in enterprise environments to enforce access control by restricting user actions that may pose a security risk, such as changing access to certain folders or downloading executable files.
68	B	A Local Group Policy is used to configure settings for systems that are not part of Active Directory.
69	A	Group Policy can control an object's script for logging on and off the system, folder redirection, Internet Explorer settings, and Windows Registry settings (the registry is a database that stores settings and options for the operating system).
70	C	Account expiration can be explicit, in that the account expires on a set date, or it can be based on a specific number of days of inactivity.
71	D	In a Windows environment, time-of-day restrictions can be set through Group Policy.
72	B	Orphaned accounts are user accounts that remain active after an employee has left an organization.
73	C	A dormant account is one that has not been accessed for a lengthy period of time.
74	D	The term account expiration indicates when an account is no longer active.
75	B	Password expiration sets the time when a user must create a new password in order to access his account.
76	C	Dormant accounts that are left unchecked can provide an avenue for an attacker to exploit without the fear of the actual user or a system administrator noticing.
77	D	A strong password should be a minimum of 15 characters in length.
78	C	One way to make passwords stronger is to use nonkeyboard characters.
79	B	Good credential management includes password protecting the ROM BIOS.

Question	Answer	Explanation
80	A	Password management applications allow users to create and store multiple strong passwords in a single user "vault" file that is protected by one strong master password.
81	B	In a Microsoft Windows Group Policy environment, the enforce password history setting determines the number of unique new passwords a user must use before an old password can be reused.
82	C	The password policy setting *maximum password age* determines how many days a password can be used before the user is required to change it.
83	D	The password policy setting *minimum password length* determines the minimum number of characters a password can have.
84	A	The password policy setting *minimum password age* determines how many days a new password must be kept before the user can change it (from 0 to 999).
85	B	The password policy setting *store passwords using reversible encryption* provides support for applications that use protocols which require knowledge of the user's password for authentication purposes.
86	D	The password policy setting *passwords must meet complexity requirements* determines whether the following are used in creating a password: Passwords cannot contain the user's account name or parts of the user's full name that exceed two consecutive characters; must contain characters from three of the following four categories—English uppercase characters (A through Z), English lowercase characters (a through z), digits (0 through 9), and nonalphabetic characters (!, $, #, %).
87	D	The password policy setting *reset account lockout counter after* determines the length of time before the account lockout threshold setting resets to zero.
88	A	The password policy setting *account lockout threshold* determines the number of failed login attempts before a lockout occurs.
89	C	The password policy setting *account lockout duration* determines the length of time a locked account remains unavailable before a user can try to log in again.
90	A	The password policy setting *account lockout threshold* has a recommended setting of 30 invalid attempts.

A

6.0

CRYPTOGRAPHY

Question	Answer	Explanation
1	B	Cryptography is the science of transforming information into a secure form so that unauthorized persons cannot access it.
2	A	Whereas cryptography scrambles a message so that it cannot be understood, steganography hides the existence of the data.
3	D	Changing the original text into a secret message using cryptography is known as encryption.
4	B	Plaintext data is cleartext data that is to be encrypted and is the result of decryption as well. Plaintext may be considered as a special instance of cleartext.
5	D	In information technology, non-repudiation is the process of proving that a user performed an action, such as sending an email message.
6	C	Whereas a stream cipher works on one character at a time, a block cipher manipulates an entire block of plaintext at one time.
7	A	A stream cipher is fast when the plaintext is short, but can consume much more processing power if the plaintext is long.
8	A	A hash algorithm creates a unique "digital fingerprint" of a set of data and is commonly called hashing.
9	D	Hashing creates a value, but it is not possible to determine the original set of data.
10	B	Symmetric cryptographic algorithms use the same single key to encrypt and decrypt a document.
11	A	Symmetric encryption is also called private key cryptography.
12	C	A completely different approach from symmetric cryptography is asymmetric cryptographic algorithms, also known as public key cryptography. Asymmetric encryption uses two keys instead of only one.

A

Question	Answer	Explanation
13	A	Proof of the sender's identity can be provided with asymmetric cryptography by creating a digital signature, which is an electronic verification of the sender.
14	B	Because mobile devices are limited in terms of computing power due to their smaller size, elliptic curve cryptography (ECC) offers security that is comparable to other asymmetric cryptography but with smaller key sizes. This can result in faster computations and lower power consumption.
15	D	Quantum cryptography attempts to use the unusual and unique behavior of microscopic objects to enable users to securely develop and share keys as well as to detect eavesdropping.
16	C	Despite the fact that asymmetric cryptography allows two users to send encrypted messages using separate public and private keys, it does not completely solve the problem of sending and receiving keys (key exchange), such as exchanging a symmetric private key. One solution is to make the exchange outside of the normal communication channels, called out-of-band.
17	C	The Diffie-Hellman (DH) key exchange requires Alice and Bob to each agree upon a large prime number and related integer. Those two numbers can be made public, yet Alice and Bob, through mathematical computations and exchanges of intermediate values, can separately create the same key.
18	A	Ephemeral keys are temporary keys that are used only once and then discarded.
19	D	Public key systems that generate random public keys that are different for each session are called perfect forward secrecy.
20	B	Key escrow refers to a process in which keys are managed by a third party, such as a trusted CA.
21	D	An HMAC is a hash-based message authentication code in which a hash function is applied to both the key and the message. HMAC is widely used by Internet security protocols to verify the integrity of transmitted data during secure communications.
22	C	Message Digest 5 (MD5), the current MD version and a revision of MD4, was created and designed to address MD4's weaknesses.
23	C	SHA-2 actually is comprised of six variations: SHA-224, SHA-256, SHA-384, SHA-512, SHA-512/224, and SHA-512/256 (the last number indicates the length in bits of the digest that is generated).

Question	Answer	Explanation
24	B	In 2007, an open competition for a new SHA-3 hash algorithm was announced. In late 2012, the final winner of the competition was announced. The winning algorithm, Keccak (pronounced catch-ack), was created by four security researchers from Italy and Belgium. Keccak will become NIST's SHA-3 hash algorithm.
25	B	Whirlpool is a relatively recent cryptographic hash function. Named after the first galaxy recognized to have a spiral structure, it creates a digest of 512 bits.
26	A	The primary design feature of RIPEMD is two different and independent parallel chains of computation, the results of which are then combined at the end of the process.
27	A	The predecessor of DES was a product originally called Lucifer, which was designed in the early 1970s by IBM and had a key length of 128 bits. The key was later shortened to 56 bits and renamed DES.
28	D	DES is a block cipher. It divides plaintext into 64-bit blocks and then executes the algorithm 16 times.
29	A	Triple Data Encryption Standard (3DES) is designed to replace DES. As its name implies, 3DES uses three rounds of encryption instead of just one.
30	B	Rijndael, more often referred to as AES, is now the official standard for encryption by the U.S. government.
31	C	RC4 is a stream cipher that accepts keys up to 128 bits in length.
32	D	The International Data Encryption Algorithm (IDEA) is a block cipher that processes 64 bits with a 128-bit key with 8 rounds. It is generally considered to be secure.
33	D	Blowfish is a block cipher algorithm that operates on 64-bit blocks and can have a key length from 32 to 448 bits.
34	C	A later derivation of Blowfish known as Twofish is also considered to be a strong algorithm, although it has not been used as widely as Blowfish.
35	B	A one-time pad (OTP) combines plaintext with a random key. It is the only known method to perform encryption that cannot be broken mathematically.

A

Question	Answer	Explanation
36	A	RSA is the most common asymmetric cryptography algorithm and is the basis for several products.
37	C	NTRUEncrypt uses a different foundation than prime numbers (RSA) or points on a curve (ECC). Instead, it uses lattice-based cryptography that relies on a set of points in space.
38	D	Elliptic Curve Diffie–Hellman (ECDH) uses elliptic curve cryptography instead of prime numbers in its computation.
39	A	Whereas DH uses the same keys each time, Diffie-Hellman Ephemeral (DHE) uses different keys.
40	B	One of the most widely used asymmetric cryptography systems for files and email messages on Windows systems is a commercial product called Pretty Good Privacy (PGP).
41	B	A similar PGP program known as GNU Privacy Guard (GPG) is an open-source product. GPG versions run on Windows, UNIX, and Linux operating systems. Messages encrypted by PGP can generally be decrypted by GPG and vice versa.
42	A	PGP uses RSA for protecting digital signatures.
43	B	Developed by Netscape in 1994 in response to the growing concern over Internet security, the design goal of SSL was to create an encrypted data path between a client and a server that could be used on any platform or operating system.
44	D	Over time updates to SSL were released. Today SSL version 3.0 is the version most web servers support.
45	D	SSL v3.0 served as the basis for TLS v1.0 (and is sometimes erroneously called SSL 3.1).
46	A	A cipher suite is a named combination of the encryption, authentication, and message authentication code (MAC) algorithms that are used with SSL and TLS.
47	C	Keys of less than 2048 bits are considered weak, keys of 2048 bits are considered good, while keys of 4096 bits are strong.
48	C	Secure Shell (SSH) is an encrypted alternative to the Telnet protocol that is used to access remote computers.
49	C	SSH is actually a suite of three utilities—slogin, ssh, and scp— that are secure versions of the unsecure UNIX counterpart utilities.

Question	Answer	Explanation
50	B	One common use of TLS and SSL is to secure Hypertext Transport Protocol (HTTP) communications between a browser and a web server. This secure version is actually "plain" HTTP sent over SSL or TLS and is called Hypertext Transport Protocol Secure (HTTPS).
51	A	IPsec encrypts and authenticates each IP packet of a session between hosts or networks.
52	D	Transport mode encrypts only the data portion (payload) of each packet yet leaves the header unencrypted.
53	A	By encrypting the packets, IPsec ensures that no other parties were able to view the contents. Confidentiality is achieved through the Encapsulating Security Payload (ESP) protocol. ESP supports authentication of the sender and encryption of data.
54	C	As the IEEE worked on the 802.11i standard, the Wi-Fi Alliance grew impatient and decided that wireless security could no longer wait. In October 2003, it introduced its own Wi-Fi Protected Access (WPA).
55	B	The heart and soul of WPA is a newer encryption technology called Temporal Key Integrity Protocol (TKIP).
56	D	Authentication for WPA Personal is accomplished by using a preshared key (PSK).
57	D	WPA2 is based on the final IEEE 802.11i standard and is almost identical to it.
58	A	The Extensible Authentication Protocol (EAP) was created as a more secure alternative than the weak Challenge-Handshake Authentication Protocol (CHAP) and Password Authentication Protocol (PAP).
59	C	LEAP is a proprietary EAP method developed by Cisco Systems and is based on the Microsoft implementation of CHAP.
60	B	PEAP is designed to simplify the deployment of 802.1x by using Microsoft Windows logins and passwords.
61	C	Digital certificates make it possible for Alice to verify Bob's claim that the key belongs to him and prevent a man-in-the-middle attack that impersonates the owner of the public key.
62	A	A Certificate Authority (CA) serves as the trusted third-party agency that is responsible for issuing the digital certificates.

A

Question	Answer	Explanation
63	C	A subscriber requesting a digital certificate first generates the public and private keys. Next, she generates a Certificate Signing Request (CSR).
64	D	A Certificate Revocation List (CRL) is a list of certificate serial numbers that have been revoked.
65	B	PKI is a framework for all of the entities involved in digital certificates for digital certificate management—including hardware, software, people, policies, and procedures—to create, store, distribute, and revoke digital certificates. In short, PKI is digital certificate management.
66	B	Public key cryptography standards (PKCS) are a numbered set of PKI standards that have been defined by the RSA Corporation.
67	A	The hierarchical trust model assigns a single hierarchy with one master CA called the root.
68	D	The bridge trust model is similar to the distributed trust model in that there is no single CA that signs digital certificates. However, with the bridge trust model there is one CA that acts as a "facilitator" to interconnect all other CAs.
69	B	In key escrow, the private key is split and each half is encrypted. The two halves are registered and sent to the third party, which stores each half in a separate location.
70	A	Key recovery agent (KRA) is a highly trusted person responsible for recovering lost or damaged digital certificates.